The Chronicles of Tiddly Cove P.D.

Stuart Leishman

Copyright © 2017 Stuart Leishman

Cover design and page layout by coversbykaren.com

Contents

Prologue.	5
Ted Scott Meets a Skunk!	8
The Texas Two Step	11
Bull Shit Baffles Brains	14
Electronic Surveillance – Oops!	17
Watch The Light!	20
Go Forth and Multiply	23
It Is Not Who You Know	26
Humour In The Face Of Sadness	29
The Body Beater	33
A Gun in the Lunch Bag	36
Gucci Holsters	40
The Exploding Volkswagen	42
Seeking the "Mindermast"	46
Not a Trained Killer	49
Police Shootings	51
Detecting 101	57
If the Shoe Fits!	61
The Mossad visits West Vancouver.	67
The One That Got Away – Almost!	70
Eric Valois – A Well-Travelled Criminal.	80
Police and the Mentally ill.	89
Gerry, a Sandwich Short of a Picnic!	92
The Death of Grace Theodorou	94
Death Has Many Faces.	98
Barricaded Suspects.	101
Drugs plus Sex plus a Contract Killer plus a Naïve Police Officer.	105
The Motorcycle Bandit.	107
Conclusion	132
About the Author	133

Prologue.

I WAS A MEMBER of the West Vancouver Police Department for almost thirty years. Working in the patrol section and ultimately in the Detective office my experiences were very broad and ranged from wrestling a cow on a local beach to investigating criminal gangs of shoplifters affiliated with the Hells Angels, investigating child sexual abuse, international extortion, robbery and murder!

The WVPD started its existence on 7th May 1912 when the newly formed District of West Vancouver, located in British Columbia on Canada's West Coast, appointed John Teare as a Police Constable. In what appeared to be a very rapid promotional system, he was appointed Chief Constable on 23rd July 1912. However, Council minutes of his appointment noted that it was to be without salary, which would explain the lack of competition!

By 1st October 1912 things were looking up for John Teare as Council awarded him a monthly salary of $75.00. However, for this princely sum he was given the added responsibilities of being the Health Officer, the Pound Keeper and the Licence Inspector. He resigned as West Vancouver's first Police Chief on 30th June 1916 when he joined the Military Police.

John Teare first Police Chief in West Vancouver

The next Chief Constable was Frank Squires who was followed by Albert Kruger and then Charlie Hailstone. Charlie was born in

Sandford Weldon, England and retired as Chief Constable in 1955. As a young constable I had the pleasure of meeting Charlie while investigating some burglaries in his apartment block in West Vancouver. He made us a pot of tea and I enjoyed listening to some of his stories as he relived his time as a West Vancouver Police Officer. He lived to celebrate the 75th Anniversary of the W.V.P.D in 1987 and died at age 91 in 1990. Moir MacBrayne succeeded Charlie Hailstone and was the man who hired me in 1973. My career spanned five Chief Constables.

On September 1st 1973 I entered the West Vancouver Police Station at 06.30 hours. A nervous young man embarking on a new career. I was very quickly put at ease by the Duty Sergeant, Jack Ross. He invited me to "Come on in, your one of us now!" Jack Ross was my mentor through much of my career. He was my first patrol Sergeant and was the Staff Sergeant in charge of the Detective Office when I was first promoted to the rank of Detective. Jack had been a member of the Royal Canadian Mounted Police and then the Winnipeg Police before moving to the West Coast and joining W.V.P.D. Until he retired at the rank of Deputy Chief Constable, he was a great influence of my career. He taught me the basics of investigations and to recognize the importance of each case to its victim, no matter how small it may appear to be. The phrase, "Without fear or favour", is frequently used but Jack Ross taught me the real meaning of it.

In 2014 I published an eBook on Amazon Kindle called "The Beat Goes On" and then in 2016 my second book, "The Detectives" was published, also an eBook on Kindle. This book is a combination of those two eBooks but with additional stories.

West Vancouver, a suburb of Vancouver, is a community situated on Canada's West Coast, sandwiched between the Pacific Ocean and soaring mountains. In its early days West Vancouver was populated by predominately English Immigrants. However, it is now inhabited by people from around world and of all ethnic backgrounds – most of whom are very wealthy.

My book begins with some stories from my early career in the patrol division. Many are humorous and humour is how many police officers dealt with the seamier side of life that we were often faced with. Sides of life that the general public often prefer not to see. Later in the book I will take you through my experiences as a Detective.

While I thoroughly enjoyed my entire police career I must confess to being happiest while working in the Detective Office. I was lucky enough to have good bosses who included Jack Ross, Gunther Wahl, Glenn Mackenzie, Frank Aikenhead, Henry Indra and Ed Pruner among others. They encouraged me to dig deep when I encountered difficult cases and supported me when I needed it. Barbara Jeffcoatt, the secretary (The person who was really in charge) in the Criminal Investigation Division, (CID) turned my illiterate reports into readable documents and kicked me out of the office to get some lunch when I was unable to tear myself away from my desk. Throughout the years I worked in CID, I worked with a large number of hardworking detectives, too many to name but Colin McKay, who you will read about later in the book, was the best partner that I could have wished for. Finally I would be remiss if I did not mention my good friend Les Fox. We were close friends throughout my police career and many of his antics still bring a smile to my face.

Detecting 101 will tell you about my early days as an investigator and some of the humorous things that happened. But then I write about more serious events, the major crimes that a detective works to solve. Robbery, International criminals and of course murder! I have included photographs and copies of some evidentiary documents that you may find interesting.

I hope you enjoy the book and I have included an email address at the end at which you can contact me. I would love to hear your comments, suggestions and if you have any questions about any of the investigations that I have written about, I would be delighted to answer them, if I can.

Stuart Leishman

Ted Scott Meets a Skunk!

THROUGHOUT THIS BOOK I will introduce you to other members of the W.V.P.D. that I worked with.

Ted Scott, the man on the cover of this book, was born on a farm in Chilliwack during a heavy snow storm on December 4th 1922. The Doctor who delivered Ted had to travel to the farm by sleigh.

In June 1941 the Second World War was being fought and Scott joined the Royal Canadian Air Force. Following his basic training he was sent to Trenton, Ontario where he received additional training and became a member of the Military Police. This started a career in Law Enforcement that would last most of his working life.

Following his discharge from the armed forces in 1945 Ted Scott tried his hand at various job opportunities before being drawn back to police work in June 1950. At that time he joined the British Columbia Provincial Police. When he joined the Provincial Force he did not receive any formal training and on his first day on the job he was handed a box containing his uniform, a gun and other pieces of equipment.

However, this was to be a short term career for Scott as within 50 days of joining the Provincial Force, it was taken over the Royal Canadian Mounted Police and Scott was transformed into a "Mountie". He earned the distinction of being the last member of the BC Provincial Police to be hired before they ceased to exist.

Due to his lack of formal training, Ted requested and received the basic training provided by the R.C.M.P. While on that course one of his troop mates was Joe Hornell. Hornell would later become the Chief Constable of the West Vancouver Police, in fact he was the Chief there when Ted Scott retired.

Following his training with the R.C.M.P., Scott was sent back to British Columbia where he served in New Westminster, Surrey and North Vancouver. One down side of being a member of the Mounted Police was that you could not marry until you had five years' service with the force. Scott had met the love of his life and with only three years of service, he decided to look elsewhere. He was hired by the

West Vancouver Police in 1953 by the then Chief Constable, Charlie Hailstone, who had a force of six men working for him.

As the police force grew in size most new members were drawn from other police organizations. Some like Tony Gage and Larry Mortimer, came from as far away as the London Metropolitan Police in England while others came from the R.C.M.P., Edmonton City Police and Calgary City Police while others such as Jack Ross came from Winnipeg City Police.

The diversity of their experience combined to make a modern and efficient force and Scott witnessed this development under three Chief Constables. Charlie Hailstone, Moir MacBrayne and Joe Hornell. Despite the growth of the organization, West Vancouver still maintained its unique style as the following story illustrates.

Scott has many stories about his police service but this one typifies the man and the police department he served with for so long. The men and women of the W.V.P.D. have long prided themselves on the fact that "no call is too small". The following story depicts that level of service.

While wildlife still surrounds West Vancouver and on occasion strays into residential areas, in years gone by there was much more interaction with wildlife. Consequently, Ted Scott became the man to call when residents and native wildlife crossed each other's path. Being an outdoorsman he frequently dealt with black bears, deer and other species. This enabled him to respond to problems with unique solutions. However, he was about to be tested like never before. A family living in the British Properties called police to report that a skunk had taken up residence in the clothes dryer. The proper screening for the outside door was not in place and Pepe le Pew had entered the kitchen and decided the drum of the clothes dryer would be a good place to settle in for the winter.

The call went out for Ted Scott and he responded, if not with great joy, at least with determination. Gingerly opening the dryer door, Scott confirmed that a skunk had indeed moved into the dryer. He gently closed the door and asked the homeowner to bring him a 2X4 piece of lumber, some string and a piece of bacon. He rubbed the bacon over the end of the 2X4 and then tied the string to the piece of bacon. Gently opening the dryer door he slowly pushed the piece of wood into the dryer with the bacon on it. The skunk began to show an interest in the bacon and as it approached, Scott pulled the string drawing the bacon out of the dryer with the skunk following it.

In what was a very delicate operation, Scott slowly backed out of the kitchen pulling the bacon, with the skunk in "hot pursuit" of its breakfast. Outside on the deck the skunk was brushing against Scott's leg as he threw the bacon towards the garden. Pepe le Pew grabbed the bacon and was seen running away towards the bush with a piece of string dragging behind him. Anyone who has smelled an area sprayed by a skunk knows the dedication to duty shown by Ted Scott. It was truly above and beyond the call of duty!

Scott eventually retired from the West Vancouver Police at the rank of sergeant but was not a man to laze away his days. He began a second career as a movie extra and appeared in many feature movies and made for TV specials.

The Texas Two Step

THE DUTIES OF a police officer are wide ranging. However, when I joined the West Vancouver Police Department in 1973, I did not realize how wide that range could be. One summers evening while I was working the night shift, a call was received at the police department about a herd of cattle swimming off Ambleside Beach!

We later learned that an investor had raised some beef cattle on one of the Gulf, Islands situated off British Columbia on Canada's West Coast and had decided to cash in his investment. He hired a tug and barge to bring the cattle from the grazing grounds to Vancouver from where they were to be transported by truck to their final destination.

As the tug entered the First Narrows and was about to sail under the Lions Gate Bridge, it encountered some rough water causing the cattle to become restless. The only thing keeping the cattle on the flat top barge was a single strand of rope that was strung around the edges. When one of the steers decided he was going to get off, there was not much to stop him. After the first one "jumped ship", the rest thought this was a good idea and all the cattle followed! Some drowned and were washed up on the beaches of Stanley Park while others were coming ashore in various areas and causing mayhem.

A passing tug found one of the cattle. They put a line on it and brought it to the nearest point of land which was a pebble beach at the foot of Radcliffe Avenue in West Vancouver. As I was the patrol officer for that area I was dispatched to deal with it. However, I was not given any guidance as to what to do with this member of the bovine species. On my arrival at the seashore, the deckhand from the tug threw me a line. I found a tired steer at the end of it. I led my new friend up onto the beach and as we stood there, deciding what to do with each other, people started arriving. Other police officers had helpful suggestions, such as where we could find a BBQ.

Members of the public from adjacent homes began wandering down in their nightclothes to see what all the fuss was about. As I discussed our options with Debbie, the manager of the local SPCA,

I was still holding the rope that was around the steer's neck. At this point one of the neighbors who had come to the beach thought it would be a good time to take a photograph.

When the flash went off, so did the steer. As it charged up the beach I was not able to slow it down with the rope so I threw my arms around its neck and dug my heels into the sand. Our local photographer thought this would make a good shot and the flash went off again, which succeeded in propelling the steer even faster up the beach. I managed to wrestle it to the ground but it was fighting to get back up when a local vet arrived and gave the steer an injection to calm it down.

Constable Leishman learns how to do the Texas Two Step.

As the steer settled down and I caught my breath, I thought we had the problem solved. But it was not to be. The steer went down on its side and lost consciousness. The vet explained that the beast was exhausted from its ordeal and that the tranquilizer had knocked it out completely. It was at about this time that I noticed the tide was coming in!

A call went out to the West Vancouver Fire Department and a rescue truck came to the beach to survey my problem. We eventually got a sheet of plywood under the steer and, with the help of the firefighters, we dragged it up to the high tide mark. By this time it was 5 a.m. and everyone was losing interest. As they all drifted away I became conscious of the cold seeping through my saltwater soaked uniform. I had to stay and wait for the owner of the steer to come and claim it, but a Good Samaritan was about to cheer me up. The neighbour who had taken the photographs came back to the beach and he gave me a cup of hot steaming coffee. As I sipped this welcome drink, I detected a strong taste of rum and being a police officer still on duty, I could not consume alcohol. However, as I continued to sip the hot beverage, I marvelled at modern science being able to make a cup of coffee taste like a hot rum toddy!

Stuart Leishman and Debbie, the S.P.C.A. manager, greet a visitor to West Vancouver.

The owner of the swimming steer arrived shortly before 7 a.m. and took custody of his property.

It was difficult not to think of my new friend for the next little while when I ordered a cheeseburger at the White Spot restaurant, but I got over it!

Bull Shit Baffles Brains

WHEN POLICE OFFICERS are checking a person or vehicle and it is declared a Code 5 situation, this signifies a danger to the investigating officers.

Through modern police training techniques Code 5 checks have evolved to a fine art, which emphasizes not only the safety of police officers and civilians in the area, but also of the suspect.

This was not always the case! One of the earliest Code 5 situations in Canadian police history was in 1885 when Superintendent Sam Steele of the North West Mounted Police faced down a mob of angry striking railroad workers.

The strikers were owed months of unpaid wages and the Federal Government was dragging its feet in addressing the situation, Sound familiar? The police, caught in the middle, asked the strikers to be patient and warned Ottawa that a riot could happen if the workers' demands were not met.

A mob estimated at 1200 workers, some armed with rifles and pistols, threatened to stop the work of non-striking workers and Steele ordered his four Mounties to arrest the strike leader and to shoot anyone who interfered. Things came to a head when the police carried their prisoner across a bridge to the jail, pursued by hundreds of armed angry workers ready to pounce.

Steele levelled his Winchester rifle at the mob and warned them that he would shoot the first man who stepped on the bridge. His determination worked and the mob backed off.

Many years later when I joined the West Vancouver Police Department, shooting the leaders of angry or dangerous mobs had been taken off the table as an acceptable police tactic!

However, actual police training with such situations had not progressed much. My first exposure to that sort of situation was early in my career when I was assigned to be the "West End" car. That meant everything from the Caulfeild area of West Vancouver to Sunset Marina on Highway 99 was my responsibility.

Following an evening break at the police station, the radio

dispatcher told me that a large group of outlaw bikers were creating a disturbance at the Horseshoe Bay ferry terminal. It turned out to be a group called the 101 Knights, based in Nanaimo on Vancouver Island. They have since affiliated with the Hells Angels.

The other police officers on duty that evening were all tied up executing a search warrant at the 303 Motel, which is now Earls Restaurant on Marine Drive in West Vancouver, the exact opposite end of the District. Consequently my supervisor, Sergeant Jack Ross, said he would come with me on the call. As we drove down into Horseshoe Bay I had no idea what to expect, with less than a year on the job I had never dealt with an outlaw motorcycle gang.

I was also keenly aware of the fact that once in Horseshoe Bay, we lost all radio contact with the police office due to a dead spot in our communications system. After parking the patrol car we walked into the ferry terminal where a group of approximately 20 hairy, leather clad goons were gathered around their Harley Davidsons. Another six or seven were racing their motorcycles up and down the parking lot.

At 5-foot ten and 140 pounds, I felt insignificant, but followed in the footsteps of Sergeant Ross who strode up to the group without hesitation. He singled out the group leader and told him in no uncertain terms that he had a group of officers waiting at the top of the hill and if things did not settle down immediately he would summon them to the terminal and "we would kick some ass!"

I furtively glanced over my shoulder wondering where this phantom group of officers had come from. The "full and frank" exchange of views that Sergeant Ross had with the bikers had the desired effect. They settled down and meekly waited in line until the ferry left.

As we drove back to the office, Jack chuckled as he explained to me that in many instances "bullshit baffles brains." There had not been many brains in that group!

Almost 20 years later, I had my own confrontation with a group of Hells Angels in that same parking lot. Now a sergeant myself, I was the duty NCO (non-commissioned officer) when the Nanaimo RCMP requested us to check a group of bikers that had been involved in an assault in their area. As the Hells Angels rode off the ferry I stood in the middle of the road with my hand up and ordered them to the side of the road.

However, in this instance, I was accompanied by several constables armed with shotguns, two detectives and an identification officer who recorded the stop on video. I thought back to that night when Sergeant Ross confronted the bikers backed up only by a 140 pound rookie and realized, it was just not the same!

Electronic Surveillance – Oops!

As EDWARD SNOWDEN, the former CIA analyst has made very clear, electronic surveillance in the 21st Century is a very sophisticated business. Satellites that circle the world can read writing on the side of vehicles, individuals can be tracked by their cellular telephones and listening devices can be placed in such a way that it is virtually impossible to detect them. Anything that is done on a computer can be tracked and/or retrieved at any time, even years in to the future.

Wiretaps and listening devices have been around for many years, but were often crude in their early days.

When I became a police officer in the early 1970s, the technology and the law dealing with wiretaps was just beginning to change. In Canada, prior to the introduction of legislation that governed the interception of private communications, police officers were able to plant bugs and intercept communications with impunity. However, the equipment to do the job and methods of installing it left much to be desired.

If the investigators were lucky, their target lived in an apartment block and it was relatively easy to gain access to what was called the "telephone room." Usually located in the basement, this room contained all the wiring for telephones going to each suite. Once the right connection had been found, alligator clips were attached and wires then ran to a reel to reel tape recorder, which was activated when the telephone receiver was picked up. The art of this type of interception lay in how well the wires and tape recorder could be concealed.

When a single-family house was the target, climbing telephone poles was often required. After finding the correct line and making the connection, again lines had to run to a location that would conceal a tape recorder. The police officers that performed these tasks learned on the job and had to employ a lot of ingenuity to accomplish their assignment. Once the tap was in place, the tapes had to be checked on a regular basis and new tapes put on the machine as required. Crooks were aware of the systems employed by the police and employed their own counter measures.

A common one of the day was to lift up the telephone handset when they were going to bed and say something like "Good night asshole," they would then leave the telephone off the hook. This would result in the recorder running all night until the reel ran out of tape.

With the introduction of legislation that allowed the police to intercept private communications came improvements on the technical side. Once a police officer had an authorization, a telephone company would look after the interception and the lines were established in monitoring rooms at the police station. However, even this was not fool- proof, as the following story will illustrate.

A local drug dealer was making arrangements to bring a shipment of narcotics from the United States into Canada and he was conducting most of his business by telephone from his apartment that was several blocks away from the West Vancouver police station. West Vancouver detectives obtained the required authorization and his telephone was bugged. The line was connected to tape recorders in the intercept room at the police office and after the suspect made a telephone call an investigator would play the tape on a backup or "slave" recorder. Now the secret to doing this successfully, with the equipment of the day, was to unplug the "slave" recorder from the telephone line, leaving the main recorder connected. But one day, an eager detective played the tape back after the suspect had hung up without unplugging the line. The suspect picked up his telephone to make another call and found himself listening to the call he had just made minutes earlier!

The final part of the story illustrates that no matter how many dumb mistakes the cops make, the crook can be even stupider. After listening to his telephone call, the drug dealer called his connection in the United States, still on the bugged line. He told his contact that he thought his line was bugged and that any further calls would be conducted on his "office telephone."

Some discreet surveillance revealed that his office telephone was a public pay phone close to his home. Consequently the authorization was widened to include that telephone. In due course our villain was arrested with the drugs and went to jail. The detective in the intercept room took a lot of ribbing for his error but he continued his successful career, a wiser man!

Watch The Light!

POLICE ORGANIZATIONS ARE like any other segment of society. They are made up of a diverse cross-section of the community they serve. West Vancouver has always had many characters and they include some people in the police department.

Taylor Way and Marine Drive has always been a busy intersection. Until recent years the traffic lights were manually controlled during the morning rush hour.

Several years ago the system was completely automated. Prior to that, a bylaw officer was in the control box each morning regulating the traffic flow and ensuring an equal amount of vehicles from Taylor Way and from Marine Drive were able to access the Lions Gate Bridge in an alternating fashion.

The late Des Hewitt, a West Vancouver bylaw officer manned the lights every morning from 1973 until his retirement.

Prior to Hewitt, police constables performed this duty and, at times, came into conflict with less-than patient drivers. The usual routine was to allow a certain number of vehicles that were eastbound on Marine Drive and then allow an equal amount that were southbound on Taylor Way.

Prior to the control box being modernized in the early 1980s, the constable on duty would walk out of the box and with an upraised hand, stop southbound traffic on Taylor Way. He would return to the box and once the traffic had cleared the intersection, he would change the light to red for Taylor Way and make it green for Marine Drive.

This system worked well, with the exception of the occasional driver who would sneak through the intersection while the constable walked back to the box. Most constables would ignore this "pushing in", as it was hard to enforce without the officer abandoning his post and running along Marine Drive towards the Lions Gate Bridge in pursuit of the offender.

However, Constable Ed Fydirchuk was not about to allow this on his watch!

Fydirchuk had noted that on one morning when he had stopped a car going south on Taylor Way that that car had gone through the intersection as he returned to the box. He made a mental note of the vehicle and watched for it each morning that week.

Whenever he saw that vehicle coming, he would stop the one in front of it and change the traffic flow to Marine Drive. The car in front would block the offending driver, who was then like a captive audience member and could not cheat his way through the intersection.

The driver quickly realized what was going on and became increasingly frustrated. He hurled abuse at Fydirchuk from his car while the constable studiously ignored him.

One morning towards the end of the week, the driver reached the end of his tether. After Fydirchuk had returned to the box and given the eastbound traffic on Marine Drive the green light, the driver got out of his car and stormed over towards the control box. The officer saw him coming and switched the traffic lights so Marine Drive had a red light and Taylor Way had a green light. This resulted in the cars stuck behind the angry driver's car blasting their horns and shouting at him to move. He had to run back to his car and he drove through the intersection glaring at Constable Fydirchuk.

The driver was greeted by the sight of the officer raising his right hand with his middle finger extended upwards in what the driver thought was an obscene gesture. The frustrated driver, a local businessman, on arrival at his office immediately telephoned West Vancouver Police Chief Moir MacBrayne to register a complaint.

When Fydirchuk returned to the police station he was summoned to see the Chief Constable who demanded an explanation for the upraised digit directed at the irate taxpayer. Fydirchuk explained to the Chief that he was just signaling the motorist to "watch the light! A true story.

I recently bumped into Ed Fydirchuk and mentioned that I had included this story in my eBook. He chuckled and told me that there were other memorable moments at those traffic lights. He related how one morning while in the control box, a motorist decided that he had waited long enough and began sounding his horn in a long steady blast. This was in an era when you did not need to release the hood from inside the car but could do it at the front of the vehicle. Cst. Fydirchuk walked over to the noisy vehicle and lifted up the car hood. He reached down to the horn and ripped out the wires. He then walked to the driver's door and dropped the wires through the window onto the driver's lap. "That's what the problem was" he told the astounded motorist and walked back to the control box to loud applause from the surrounding vehicles. Of course, this indeed was another era. Today he would be recorded on a cell phone camera and it would be posted on Facebook. The civil liberties brigade would be up in open arms and the police complaint authorities would have a field day. But, happily this was not the case in those days and a rude motorist was taught a lesson I am sure he did not forget in a hurry. This was how Cst. Fydirchuk dealt with "Road Rage".

Go Forth and Multiply

GOOD JUDGES ARE few and far between. As a young constable I had the pleasure of appearing before provincial court Judge Perry Miller, a man who made a difference in the community he served.

During his tenure in the West Vancouver provincial court in the 1970s, there was a significant improvement in the attitude of the "local yokels" when it came to their conduct in public places and in their dealings with the constabulary.

Most lawyers were accustomed to appearing before a judge and spouting forth unmitigated claptrap on behalf of their clients, hoping for lenient treatment. In many instances they got it.

When they appeared before Judge Miller, he would sit and politely listen, smiling benignly at the lawyer and the accused. If the accused was convicted, he would then lean forward looking down intently at the person while handing down a punitive sentence, not infrequently involving a term of imprisonment.

I believe it was his demeanor in court that earned him the nickname "The Smiling Cobra" from local lawyers. The short sharp shock of being held responsible for their actions had a sobering effect on the local criminal element and on wild teenagers who thought it was their right to run amok in the community.

Word spread quickly and when constables went to disturbances in public places it was often sufficient to tell the participants to shut the party down and to disperse. In most instances this was the only action required. However, there were those who had not heard the message that a new judge was in town and they had to learn the hard way.

Constable Don Herder had moved to West Vancouver from Ontario where he had served in the Ontario Provincial Police. He was a fair man to deal with but he did not put up with any nonsense.

One evening, he was called to a local nightclub called Clyde's Disco on Marine Drive. A local youth was drunk and had been thrown out of the club by the bouncers. He was causing a disturbance in the street and despite a warning from Herder that he should go home, he continued with his drunken revelry.

As this lad was known to enjoy in engaging in fisticuffs with police officers I went to assist the constable in making the arrest. By the time I arrived the fight was on and the youth was struggling with Herder, who was trying to get a pair of handcuffs on him.

A group of youths were gathered around the two combatants and as word spread in the nightclub more spectators poured onto the street. My first task was to move the group back from the struggle. I then helped Herder to get the fighter into the back seat of the police car. The young man then began pounding the windows of the police car with his feet, threatening to break the glass so we opened the door to restrain him.

That was a mistake!

He fought his way out of the police car and we were soon all rolling in the gutter. It was at this point that a drinking buddy of the fighter decided to intervene on his friend's behalf. He began by demanding to know by what authority we were arresting his frisky pal.

As we were otherwise engaged, we ignored him and he decided to step up his level of intervention by shouting in my ear. He was successful in that he attracted my attention so I warned him that we were engaged in making an arrest and that he was obstructing us and I suggested that he "go forth and multiply"!

He backed away for a moment, but as we were getting the fighter back into the rear of the police car, the drinking buddy grabbed my shoulder and began swearing again. Within minutes he found himself handcuffed and sitting next to the fighter as we drove to the police station.

Two months later the drinking buddy appeared before Judge Perry Miller, charged with obstructing a police officer. As I gave my evidence I described to the court the struggle we had with the other youth and the conduct of the accused. I told the judge that I had twice warned the accused that he was obstructing us and of the consequences he faced if he continued.

When the accused took the stand, he said he had just wanted to know what was happening to his friend. He said he did not know he was obstructing us. In regards to the warning I gave him, he said "Constable Leishman just told me to fuck off."

At this point Judge Miller leaned forward over the bench, glaring at the accused, and said, "But you did not take his advice!" The accused was subsequently convicted and sentenced to 10 days in the Oakalla Prison Farm. I am sure he emerged a wiser man.

It Is Not Who You Know

THE DISTRICT OF West Vancouver has a luxury that many surrounding municipalities have not seen for many years.

It is a police department with a policy that no call is too small. This policy results in West Vancouver police officers seeing many situations that their counterparts in adjacent police organizations never encounter. Consequently, many humorous situations develop, allowing some of the characters that have been with the West Vancouver police over the years a chance to perform.

Constable Dave Marskell is no longer with the department, but during his service his sense of humour resulted in many chuckles within the organization. A number of years ago he stopped a car for speeding and when the female driver presented him with her driver's licence, he began writing out a ticket. The lady was astounded that she was getting a ticket and said to Marskell, "I am Margaret Trudeau, don't you know who I am? I am the ex-wife of the ex-prime minister." Marskell stopped writing the ticket and with a huge smile on his face, said to her, "I have a brother that lives in California."

With a puzzled look, she then asked him what that had to do with anything. Returning to his deadpan look, he replied, "Exactly" as he completed writing her speeding ticket.

I don't think that the Vancouver Police Department receives too many calls about theft of geese, but it is an offence that is not taken lightly in the District of West Vancouver.

A local lad frequently had too much to drink and got involved in all sorts of nefarious acts that kept the police department busy. One evening he decided to steal some geese from Ambleside Park. The investigators were soon on his trail and arrested him in possession of the geese. He was released into the custody of his family to sober up and the geese were held as exhibits.

Lacking any designated geese pens at the police station, the investigators put the birds into the "drunk tank" in the cell-block. Later that evening another police officer arrested a local man for being drunk in a public place and decided to hold him in custody until he was sober. As the drunk tank was "occupied" he was put in the cell directly opposite. As the drunk settled in, he became aware of the honking geese in the cell across the way. He looked at them but did not say anything and eventually fell into a sound sleep.

During the night arrangements were made to move the geese to the SPCA and they were taken from the cell while the drunk slept. When he was being released the following morning the officer noticed him looking intently at the now empty "drunk tank" and eventually the jailed man asked if anyone else had been in there during the night. The officer somberly assured him that he had been the only person in the cells that night and, with that, released him. I don't know if the experience affected his drinking habits, but the geese must have given him something to think about.

The welfare of dumb animals has always been of concern to members of the West Vancouver police. Consequently, when a dog was hit by a car and trapped in the vehicle's suspension the duty sergeant and his corporal attended to render what assistance they could.

A tow truck was at the scene and had tried lifting the car from various angles in an effort to free the whimpering dog, but without success.

Eventually, when it seemed nothing would work, Sgt. Grant Churchill made a hard decision and decided the dog should be put out of its misery. Cpl. Colin McKay would have preferred that Churchill had continued on with this display of leadership by doing the deed himself, but it was not to be. McKay was designated as the "hit man".

A small calibre firearm was brought to the scene and McKay crawled under the expensive, low slung automobile, to do his duty! As he neared the trapped animal, he tried to avoid the large brown eyes of his intended victim. He steeled himself for the task and after taking careful aim, he pulled the trigger. The bullet missed the dog, but pierced the costly Pirelli tire. As the tire lost air the dog freed itself from the suspension and reportedly "ran like hell", never to be seen again by the assembled observers.

It was a happy ending for all, except the driver of the high-end automobile, who had to explain to his insurance company how a police bullet had ruined his tire!

Humour In The Face Of Sadness

During my career as a police officer I found that humour presents itself in the most unlikely places.

During the 1980s I was a detective and investigating child sexual assault was one of my main duties, one that I took very seriously.

However, a seven year old girl, who I will call Mary, managed to have a good laugh with me during what was a traumatic time for her. In 1986 I produced a book for the West Vancouver Police Association. It was called the Child Sexual Assault Manual.

When I wrote the introduction, the following was written based on my experiences with Mary:

"Child abuse is an historical fact, from which no nation or race is free of guilt. It is only within the past one hundred years that some measure of improvement has begun to be noticed in the "Civilized" world. We can sit back content with the knowledge that the horrors of which Charles Dickens wrote, are no longer rampant in our modern society with its far reaching social programs and all-encompassing legislation."

"However, for the seven year old girl who lives in dread of the nights that Granddad comes to "babysit", there is a different perception on our world. She knows that Granddad is going to come and give her a "goodnight kiss". She does not understand why he has to take his clothes off and get into bed with her, she recoils from his touches and cries herself to sleep after he satisfies his desires."

As you can see, Mary's grandfather was sexually abusing her.

Eventually she told her parents who contacted me because the suspect was a West Vancouver resident and most of the offences had taken place in our jurisdiction. I drove to Mary's home to meet her and her parents to explain how the investigation would evolve and to assess how Mary would stand up as a witness, if the case went to court.

I explained to them that I would interview Mary at the police station and our meeting would be videotaped to minimize further interviews with her by a Crown prosecutor. I also discussed the possibility of giving evidence in court and the role of Crown and defence lawyers. During this discussion, I told Mary that I would give her a tour of the police station and the courtroom to explain where everyone would be and what they would be doing. Mary and her parents were listening intently to every word and it is at this point that I intended to say, "I will show you where the judge sits," but what I actually said was "I will show you where the judge shits."

As soon as the words passed my lips, I realized what I had said and decided to just keep talking, hoping it had been missed. Within less than a minute Mary's face broke into a large grin and her parents followed with subdued chuckles. At this point I realized I was not going to get away with the gaffe and we all had a good laugh.

Mary proved to be an excellent witness and her interview went so well that when her grandfather was confronted with the evidence on the tape, he admitted his guilt. He was sentenced to a prison term.

This little girl had a lot of guts and supportive parents. I believe she was capable of putting this terrible experience behind her.

There was one other incident in Mary's case that still makes me smile. The videotape equipment that we used in those days was bulky and the actual tape went into a VCR while the camera was connected by two cords, one for the sound and the other for visual. The whole thing was connected to a television, where we viewed the tapes. I later asked our forensic identification officer to make me a copy of the taped interview for the Crown prosecutor.

During the process, the officer confused one of the cords and when I viewed the duplicate tape, the picture on the screen showed Mary and me talking but the voices came from the cablevision audio. The voices on the tape were Big Bird and Oscar the Grouch of Sesame Street having a conversation.

If it had not been such a traumatic incident I would have given Mary a copy of the duplicate tape, but given the situation, it was a smile that I kept to myself.

During my career I investigated many cases of child sexual assault that had occurred in West Vancouver. When I began these types of investigations they were generally not handled very well by police investigators, Crown Counsel, the courts and society in general. This began to change in the early 1980s following the release of the Badgley Report which looked into the problem of child sexual abuse. Improvements began to show in all areas as to how these investigations should be handled. It was not easy being on the frontier of these changes, many elements of society fought against the more enlightened way that these crimes were investigated and prosecuted. However, I did take satisfaction in that one of the cases which I investigated had a ground breaking ruling from the BC Court of Appeal.

Michael Bennett was a social worker by profession and held a senior position with the Federal Government. Using his position as a "Big Brother" with the Big Brothers organization, he sexually molested many young boys with devastating consequences for the victims. Following my investigation, he was charged and convicted. The Judge imposed a sentence of two years less a day, which would be served in a Provincial jail. On appeal, the higher court doubled his sentence to four years in a Federal Penitentiary. This began to send the right message. However, I am saddened to see that the courts seem to be slipping back in their sentencing. The following statement made by Justice MacFarlane of the BC Court of Appeal, and endorsed by Chief Justice Nemetz and Justice Akins, should be heeded.

"We ought not to communicate the message to pedophiles that if they get caught and repent and take treatment that they will go unpunished. What the message ought to be is if they are caught and

repent and take treatment, that they may expect incarceration and, as we are proposing, a lengthy term of probation to enable the treatment to be fulfilled."

The Body Beater

DEATH FREQUENTLY TAPS police officers on the shoulder in a variety of ways. The contacts with the Grim Reaper come in many forms and in order to maintain one's sanity it is necessary to have a working relationship with this entity.

While some may find it inappropriate, I think that a sense of humour does help. My introduction to the subject of death came when I was a police recruit in training in 1973.

In those days all recruits attended an autopsy, which at that time were done in the Vancouver City Analysts' Laboratory. This building now houses the Vancouver Police Centennial Museum, just around the corner from the old police headquarters building at 312 Main Street in Vancouver.

Along with my classmates, we trooped into the analysts' laboratory with a certain amount of trepidation. I think all of us were relieved when we were told that no bodies were available that morning so we would just have a tour of the building along with a lecture. During the tour we were shown jars that contained the brain, the stomach contents and other organs of a man who had died in a knife fight in Prince George, Northern British Columbia the previous week. While it was not particularly pleasant, it did not really bother me until I got home for dinner and found that my wife had prepared liver and onions along with a healthy serving of chopped red cabbage!

Over the years I worked with pathologist Dr. Rex Farris on a number of occasions. He was an excellent pathologist and gave expert evidence at high profile cases around the world.

The first case we worked on together was a report of human remains that had been found on Black Mountain, in West Vancouver. Ferris, West Vancouver Police Identification Officer, Andy Mendel and I set out to find the body reported by a hiker.

Our first attempt to find the body was a disaster. We took a wrong turn on a mountain trail and eventually found ourselves knee deep in snow and many hundreds of feet above where we were supposed to be.

We came back the next day and tried again. This time the hiker was able to come with us and show us the spot. We found a number of human bones, body parts and a skull. We discovered the remains of a camp along with some identification. We placed all the human remains in a body bag and after completing our on scene investigation, we began our trek down the mountain.

Mendel and I were carrying the body bag and as we crossed a creek that was swollen with melting snow the bag broke, spilling its contents into the water. As we scrabbled around retrieving the bones and body parts from the creek, Ferris looked on in horror as the remains he intended to do an autopsy on were swirling away down the creek.

We did recover all the body parts and eventually learned that the dead man was a transient who lived on the mountain. He had not picked up his welfare cheque for several months. Ferris established that the dead man had a broken leg. We believed that he had fallen while walking from his camp to the creek and injured himself. He had died on the mountainside and animals had scattered his remains around.

While working with pathologists was usually associated with a suspicious death, on occasion I turned to Ferris for his expert opinion on other matters. Later in my career I was the Sergeant in the Detective Office and one of my duties was to investigate complaints made against police officers. Integrity was essential in these cases and a fine balance had to be maintained. It was equally important to thoroughly investigate every complaint made against a police officer in order to maintain public confidence and also to ensure police officers were not made scape goats on the altar of political correctness.

Police had been called to a rowdy party that got out of hand and spilled onto the street. The following day a young man came to the police station and filed a complaint against a police officer. The young man complained of being beaten with a riot stick as he was leaving the area of the party. The officer involved remembered the incident and in his statement reported that the youth had refused to leave and was encouraging other youths to ignore police directions to disperse. The officer said he used his riot stick to push the youth, moving him along. The officer further stated that he had held the stick with both hands and pushed him but did not strike him.

When I interviewed the young man I asked him to go into details about the alleged assault. He told me that the police officer had struck him across the back with the stick, in a swinging motion and that he had also struck him in the back with end of the riot stick.

I asked him to show me his back. When he took off his shirt I photographed his back which showed no sign of bruises or other marks I would have expected, given the nature of the reported assault.

It seemed obvious to me that the complaint was without merit but I thought it prudent to get an independent opinion. I took the officer's riot stick to the morgue at the Vancouver General Hospital and had a meeting with Rex Ferris. I asked him for his opinion on what sort of marks, if any, would he expect to find on the young man's back given the assault described by the youth in his statement. He pointed out the cross hatching in the wood on both ends of the stick, which is used to help the officer's grip on the stick.

It was his opinion that a swinging blow across the back would result in severe bruising and probably would show the pattern that was cut into the wood. He also told me that a strong blow with the end of the stick would result in a severe bruise that would last for several days.

This opinion helped me conclude the complaint as unfounded. When I returned to the police station, following my visit to the morgue, a detective asked me what I had been doing there with the riot stick. I described my investigation and told him that Ferris and I had been striking dead bodies with the stick to establish what marks it would make. The gullible detective turned pale and said, "My God! You are ruthless." I looked at him with a straight face and replied, "But they were dead, they didn't feel a thing." I never enlightened him to the truth and to this day he probably believes that I was beating dead bodies at the morgue.

A Gun in the Lunch Bag

As a young constable in the West Vancouver Police Department I had my first brush with "organized crime" as a result of a shoplifting call to Woodward's department store in the Park Royal Shopping Centre.

What at first blush appeared to be a minor theft and fraud ballooned into a wide ranging criminal investigation. Many police officers considered "shoplifting calls as a waste of time". However, my mentor, Sergeant Jack Ross, had taught me that all investigations were important primarily for the victim, in this case a business, and also for honing investigative skills for more major crimes that would cross my path later in my career.

Marg Emmons was the office manager of this Woodward's branch and also supervised the security personnel. Consequently, she had a nose for criminals who dared to ply their trade in her store. "Aunty Marg, as she was affectionately known, spoke to me on my arrival. She detailed how Jackie F., the young woman in the security office, had tried to obtain a refund for a sweater without a receipt, claiming it was a gift she did not want. She had given one name on the refund form, but when asked for identification, she had produced a driver's licence in another name. Between the times that Jackie F had been detained and my arrival, Auntie Marg had done a quick check on Woodward's "no bill refund file". This is a file that was maintained by department stores that had the names and addresses of people seeking refunds for merchandise without receipts. She found the two names that the young woman had presented had been used in multiple no bill refunds, totalling many hundreds of dollars.

I took Jackie F back to the police station for an interview and to begin with she refused to say anything. So I relied on the opinion of Jack Ross, that "bullshit often baffle brains".

I took an empty cardboard file folder and filled it with scrap paper until it bulged. I walked into the interview room and dropped it on the table and announced to Jackie, that we had been conducting an investigation into these frauds for some time. She turned very pale and said, "I am not going down for all those, there were other people involved."

During the interview that followed Jackie admitted that she was part of a gang that was involved in extensive theft and refund frauds throughout the Lower Mainland of Vancouver. She told me that on the day she was arrested at Woodward's she was doing a little "freelancing."

She named the head of the gang as Sandra Lynn Anderson. Sandy Anderson had an extensive criminal record and was identified as an associate of the Hells Angels motorcycle gang because her boyfriend was a biker. Because of the Hells Angels connection, I contacted a section of the Royal Canadian Mounted Police that specialized in investigating the activities of the outlaw motorcycle gangs and their associates. Sergeant Don Brown, the man in charge of that section, was very interested in the information I had gleaned from Jackie and he set about organizing a task force to deal with this group.

Brown asked the West Vancouver police department if I could be assigned to the task force because of my initial involvement. Consequently, I was re-assigned to plain clothes on a temporary basis. The task force consisted of members of the RCMP, two members of the Vancouver City Police Department, myself from West Vancouver and store security personnel from Woodward's, Eaton's and Sears. All these department stores had sustained major losses at the hands of this gang.

Anderson operated this theft ring in a business – like fashion. She had a number of helpers that she used and would "go to work", as she called it, on a daily basis. Her modus operandi was simple. She would drive to a shopping centre, go into a major department store where she would steal several expensive items such as sweaters or blouses. When she returned to the parking lot, she passed the stolen items to her assistants. These assistants would go back into the store and obtain cash refunds, claiming the items were unwanted gifts. It was estimated that Anderson was stealing approximately $200,000 (1970s dollars) of goods annually.

The first day I reported to work with the task force I was assigned to work with an RCMP corporal. As we drove to Langley to set up surveillance on Anderson's house, the corporal kept looking at my brown paper lunch bag that I was gripping tightly. He eventually asked me if I would like to throw it in the trunk. It was at this point that I sheepishly explained that my service revolver was in the bag. West Vancouver did not have any spare small side arms to give me, nor did they have a shoulder holster for the large uniform model that I had, so the lunch bag was my only alternative. This brought some good natured ribbing from the corporal and the other guys I worked with. The next day someone found a spare shoulder holster and loaned it to me.

The project went well. Anderson was a busy shopper and we had the security people from the stores follow her into the retail establishments to watch her steal the merchandise. They then waited in the store and watched the refund take place, after which they would seize the item as an exhibit and then we would go on to the next shopping mall and do it all again.

We had a number of vehicles for the surveillance but it was not easy. Sandy Anderson drove a pickup truck and while "working" she drove like a maniac in order to spot surveillance. She would have her girls sit in the back seat of the truck watching out of the back window for any following vehicles that were keeping up with her. This required some fancy driving on the part of the surveillance team. If we could anticipate where she might be going, we would put a car in front of her and where possible have other vehicles driving on parallel streets, the lead car would indicate if she turned off and the other vehicles would try and pick her up at an intersection. Occasionally we would lose her but then all the surveillance cars would fan out to surrounding shopping centres and we would eventually find her – at work!

The surveillance lasted for several weeks until we had enough evidence to link all members of the gang in the conspiracy. During this time the corporal told me many amusing stories about the biker gangs and included one about Anderson.

Anderson was a horse fancier and entered her horse in many competitions and shows. She happened to be under surveillance on another matter when she was at one of these shows and an RCMP member followed her into the horse barns. She went to a competitor's horse and while she thought no one was around, she cut off the horse's tail. The shows organizers were advised of what had taken place and this resulted in her being kicked out of the show.

At the conclusion of the investigation, as in all good organized crime stories, simultaneous pre-dawn raids were conducted to pick up all the suspects.

I was assigned to arrest Jackie F., the young woman who had started all this. Yes, despite knowing that she had told us all about the operation, she had kept her mouth shut and continued to participate! As I was making my arrest from the West Vancouver Police station I had to try and get an unmarked car to use. As with snub nosed revolvers, young constables working in plain clothes did not rank high in the pecking order.

I eventually managed to get my hands on an old Pontiac that no one else would drive. Jackie was now a resident of the Maywood Home for unwed mothers on Oak Street in Vancouver. Consequently, I was making my "pre-dawn raid" without backup. As I negotiated rush hour traffic through Vancouver streets, I wondered if I would even make it. My unmarked police car kept coughing and sputtering and, following a loud backfire, it stalled at an intersection with smoke coming from under the hood. Serpico? I think not!

Eventually I made it to the Maywood home, only to find that Jackie had left on a bus since she had a court appearance for theft in Vancouver. I managed to coax my car to the Vancouver provincial courthouse on Main Street and arrested my very pregnant suspect as she left court.

At the end of the day seven people were charged and convicted of conspiracy to commit theft and received varying terms of imprisonment and I am sure have since lived exemplary lives.

Gucci Holsters

As mentioned earlier, The District of West Vancouver is home to many wealthy people. The residents enjoy the highest per capita earnings in Canada.

However, contrary to popular belief, members of the police department did not carry Walther PPK pistols in Gucci holsters. Our handcuffs were not fur-lined and despite intensive lobbying by the Police Association, we were not able to convince the West Vancouver Police Board that Mercedes SL Roadsters were a good choice for patrol cars.

While most people who live in West Vancouver are ordinary people making a living and paying a mortgage, the high priced real estate does attract some well-heeled and in some instances famous people as residents.

One day as I drove away from the police station at 13th Street and Marine Drive, I saw an expensive sports car drive through a red light. I pulled the car over and issued the driver a traffic ticket. The driver was cooperative and gave me no reason to suspect him of anything. But as a junior and inexperienced police constable I was naïve and wondered how this guy with long hair and wearing a black leather jacket could afford his expensive sports car and own a home on Millstream Drive in the British Properties.

He must a drug trafficker, I thought! Having arrived at this stunning revelation, I returned to the police office and sought out a man of "great knowledge" to share my information with. When I described my encounter and my observations to Detective Larry Catlin, he agreed it was something that should be looked into. The following day Catlin told me that he had checked out my "suspicious character" who turned out to be Randy Bachman. He asked me if I had ever heard of the rock group, Bachman-Turner Overdrive. Catlin went onto explain that Bachman was the lead singer with this group and that his wealth was earned legitimately. I learned a valuable lesson that day on not judging a book by its cover. However, at some point I must sort through my old ticket books, I might have a valuable autograph.

On another occasion I was given a telephone number in New York and told to call it collect and speak with a Mr. Millar. It was Will Millar of the Irish Rovers singing group. Millar had been in New York on business and had not been able to contact his wife at his West Vancouver home. (What a difficult time we had before cell phones.) He asked me if I would mind checking it out, as he was concerned about his dog not being fed. I did not ask him if he would like me to feed his wife, should I come across her, but I thought she would give me guidance in that direction, should I encounter her.

I found the front door unlocked at the Millar's home and checked the house out. I did not find his wife or the dog, but I did find an Irish style bar in his basement that I would have given my right arm for. I called Millar in New York and let him know what I had done. He thanked me for my time….Remember, this was West Vancouver, "no call too small!"

Some months later I stopped a car for running a stop sign in the Westmount area of West Vancouver and found Millar was the driver. I wrote him a traffic ticket but on reflection I considered anyone who was that concerned about his dog and had such a classy bar deserved a warning.

Consequently, I made it a warning ticket. I really must go through my old ticket books in search of celebrity autographs.

The Exploding Volkswagen

HIGH SPEED CAR chases scare the hell out of police officers. No matter what the end results, you can rely on the fact that it will generate volumes of paperwork (for the officer) and if anything goes wrong the officer will be second guessed by senior police officers, lawyers, judges and any media personnel who are having a slow day.

The phrase "high speed chase" was so inflammatory in police circles that now retired West Vancouver Police Corporal Dick Clancy refused to use the expression. He preferred to say that he was involved in a "rapid following." While I had been involved in a few short high speed pursuits, my real introduction to a "knock em down, drag it out," high speed pursuit came on April 13th 1979. I had been working what had been a fairly quiet night shift.

Shortly before 3 a.m. I was sent to assist Patrolman Ernie Codrington of the now defunct BC Highway Patrol. Approximately 15 minutes earlier he had seen a man driving a pickup truck northbound through the Stanley Park Causeway in the centre lane. This lane was closed to traffic in both directions at that time of night.

Codrington stopped the truck and issued the driver a ticket. Because the driver had been drinking and showed some signs of impairment he also gave him a 24 hour driving suspension. Shortly after he saw the man driving his truck over the Lions Gate Bridge. Codrington stopped him at the Patrol office at the north end of the bridge and called for assistance from the West Vancouver Police.

When I arrived I saw the driver look over his shoulder at me and then drive away as I walked towards his truck. The patrolman shouted to me that he had given the driver a 24 hour suspension. I followed the truck eastbound on Marine Drive with my emergency lights and siren on. The driver refused to stop and continued driving along Marine Drive and entered North Vancouver. This area is policed by the RCMP and in those days we had no direct radio communication. I called my office and asked them to telephone the RCMP and to relay my radio transmissions to them. Codrington and I tried to box the truck in but he drove around us and began running red lights as he increased his speed. Mounties began to appear and roadblocks were put in place to try and stop the truck but the driver just drove around them. Up to this point, while the driver was exceeding the speed limit, driving through red lights and on the wrong side of the road his speed was not dangerously excessive.

We had driven along Marine Drive onto 3rd Street and were now going down the Cotton Street hill towards Main Street. The pickup truck was in the lead followed by me, then by Codrington and behind us several RCMP cruisers. A young Mountie decided he was going to put an end to this "parade" and he began passing everyone on the left side. When he came alongside the truck he tried to push it into the curb but the truck nudged him into the raised centre median and his left tyre exploded. We left him to begin composing his "Dear Chief" letter while the rest of us now drove onto the (then) Second Narrows Bridge. As we were entering the City of Vancouver we felt obliged to let them know and several Vancouver City Police cars joined the procession. As with the RCMP, the Vancouver Police were also on their own radio frequency so communications continued through our various dispatchers. By this time the truck was swerving across all traffic lanes and had side swiped several police cars. This incident took place before the Cassiar Street tunnel was built and as we came off the Second Narrows Bridge we continued south on Cassiar before the suspect swerved onto Rupert Street just before the (then) entrance to the Trans-Canada Highway. He then turned onto Grandview Highway and we were now westbound – and the speed had increased greatly. At this point I was directly behind the suspect truck followed by Codrington of the BC Highway Patrol, several members of the North Vancouver RCMP, a number of Vancouver City Police Cars and I later learned, a Burnaby RCMP member was in the line somewhere. To this day, I don't know where he came from.

As we travelled east on Grandview Highway the truck made a sharp right turn onto North Grandview. I managed to stay with him but the rest of the police vehicles overshot and it was just the truck and I. The truck turned north on Semlin Street as I tried to relay my position to the dispatcher. At Semlin and Broadway the truck drove through a stop sign at an estimated speed of 60 kmh. and T boned an old Volkswagen van loaded with hippies that was eastbound on Broadway.

To my horror the VW van exploded into a ball of flames flipped on its side and slid along Broadway. The suspect truck had been turned around by the impact and was now facing me across the street. The driver started to go again but I rammed my police cruiser into the truck and the chase was over.

My heart was sinking as I ran to the burning VW van, but by a miracle all the occupants had managed to get out and seemed unscathed. The driver of the pickup truck tried to leave the scene on foot but was stopped in his tracks by a Vancouver Police dog and his handler who had arrived at the scene. Coincidently, the police dog handler was my brother, Colin, who was a member of the Vancouver Police.

I later checked and found the distance travelled was 10.7 miles and had taken 17 minutes. The suspect never gave a reason for not stopping and was charged with criminal negligence on the operation of a motor vehicle. He was convicted and received a substantial prison term.

Chases such as this were as controversial then as they are now. This man had been drinking and driving and had been suspended. If I had let him drive away and he had killed or injured someone I would have been held responsible. If any of the people in the Volkswagen van had been killed or seriously injured I would have held myself responsible, so what do you do? As it turned out I did my paperwork, thanked my lucky stars that there was no disaster and went to Denny's for breakfast!

Things are different today. Guidelines restrict the number of police vehicles that can become involved to a primary and a backup. The various police departments can now communicate directly with their radios and such innovations as the "spike belt" and nail strips are available to cut short long chases. It is still a very difficult thing for police to deal with and if death or injury results it seems that society would prefer to blame the police rather than put the responsibility where it belongs, on the offenders!

Seeking the "Mindermast"

POLICE OFFICERS DEAL with a wide range of people. Some could be described as geniuses while others are as thick as gate posts.

During the 1960s, a criminal gang in England committed the robbery of a mail train and stole in excess of six millions pounds. This incident became known as "The Great Train Robbery" and the investigation was later lampooned by the great comedic team of Peter Cook and Dudley Moore in one of their "Beyond the Fringe" skits.

Peter Cook portrayed a Chief Inspector from New Scotland Yard who was being interviewed about the robbery by a BBC commentator, Dudley Moore.

At one point the Chief Inspector is asked if he knows who is behind the crime to which he responds, "We believe this to be the work of a mindermast." He went on to explain that "mindermast" is a code word used at Scotland Yard to describe a "mastermind". "We don't like to use the word "mastermind" as it depresses the men," he explained.

In real police work we seldom came across "masterminds" and, in actual fact, in most instances crooks were ferreted out by the stupid mistakes that they made.

Arson is a crime that is seldom successfully prosecuted, which is amazing when you examine some of the dumb errors made by the crooks in many arson cases.

A local media personality who was undergoing financial difficulties decided to ease the pressure by burning his boat and claiming the insurance.

When the North Vancouver Detachment of the Royal Canadian Mounted Police investigated the boat fire, witnesses told them that the boat owner had been seen walking away from the vessel shortly before it burst into flames. They reported seeing him put something into a garbage can. A police officer checked and found a container in the garbage can that had gasoline residue in it. Further investigation showed the container bore the fingerprints of the boat owner.

Analysis of the gasoline showed it was the same as the accelerant used to start the fire in the boat. Consequently, he was charged with arson.

At trial his story was that he had left his boat in good order and as he walked to his car he noticed the container laying in the parking lot. Being a "good citizen", he picked it up and placed it into the garbage can where the police later found it. While police did not think much of his story, a jury did and he was acquitted!

During the 1970s two young ladies borrowed a substantial amount of money from the local credit union in West Vancouver.

They opened a hair dressing business on Marine Drive, across the street from the police station, and when business reverses put them into dire financial straits, they decided to let the insurance company pay off the loan to the credit union.

They went into their business premises late at night and doused the entire place in gasoline. As they left through the back door they lit something to start the fire, but had not counted on the accumulation of fumes in the air and the place exploded in their faces.

Firefighters found them at the back door, reeking of gasoline with singed hair and clothing – not an easy situation for them to explain.

Following an investigation they were charged with arson but one later jumped bail and I believe returned to her native England. Her friend faced the music in Canada but she managed to shift most of the blame to her absent friend and got off pretty lightly in court.

Another case involved a unique way of profiting from a real estate deal. A man bought a house in West Vancouver, it was an older house in need of some updating. After the deal had been made the daughter of the current owners was home sick, from school. She heard some noise in the carport and looked out to see the man who had bought the property. She assumed he was just checking things out but minutes later realized the carport had erupted into a large blaze. She called the fire department and a fire fighter would later testify in court that he had seen the "buyer" hot footing it down the street away from the scene of the fire. The suspect of course denied it and claimed to have been in Vancouver at the time. Further investigation showed he had a track record of being involved in similar events. It seems he would buy older houses, set them on fire and then expect the current owner's house insurance to build him a new house. Despite the evidence of the daughter and firefighter, a jury acquitted him of arson. Reasonable doubt is a great thing but it can certainly be manipulated by competent defence lawyers.

While in the previous case, luckily the daughter of the house holder was not hurt, this next case turned tragically fatal for one of the participants.

An East European businessman owned an older house in West Vancouver and like many before him, decided he would like his insurance company to build him a new home.

He hired a young man from his native country to burn the house down while he was "out of the country on business." He made a point of placing telephone calls from the United States on the day of the fire to establish his alibi.

The young man who was going to do the deed took off all his clothes and left them in a neat pile by the backdoor. It was speculated that he did that to avoid getting gasoline fumes on them. He then walked around the house spilling liberal amounts of gasoline in various rooms. Like the hairdresser in the earlier incident, he did not count on the build-up of fumes. As he approached the backdoor of the house, it exploded into a ball of fire, killing him instantly. The source of ignition was never established but it could have been something as simple as him turning a light on or off, or the furnace cutting in.

While the real villain in this case was not prosecuted due to a lack of hard evidence, I had a quiet word in the ear of the insurance company and I believe he did have some problems with his insurance claim!

All these people thought they had a solution to their problems in life, but unfortunately for them, none of them were a "mindermast!"

Not a Trained Killer

During basic police training, the safe handling and use of a firearm was of great importance. New officers spent many hours on the range learning those skills. However, you can't teach anyone about the "blood and guts" side of a gun. That can only come from experience and I got mine within the first year on the job.

One summer's morning in the early 1970s I was dispatched to a newly completed Upper Levels portion of the Trans-Canada highway that ran through West Vancouver.

A vehicle driven by a middle-aged lady had struck a deer and the animal lay injured on the side of the road. The deer's right rear leg was clearly broken and it had sustained severe injuries in the rump. Despite my lack of veterinary training, it was clear to me the only possible course of action was to put the animal out of its misery.

Constable Peter Norman, another rookie West Vancouver Police Department officer, had arrived and he agreed it was the only thing we could do. As I took my revolver from its holster the woman driver who had struck the deer gasped and asked what I was doing.

I explained that the only option was to quickly end the animals suffering. She demanded that we call the SPCA or the Vancouver Zoo in Stanley Park and have them send someone up to tend to the deer. While I tried to explain to the women that neither of these organizations would attend, nor could they do any good given the extent of the injuries, the deer pulled itself up and dragged its injured body into the bushes at the side of the highway.

I ignored the woman's protests and followed the deer into the bush. It had again laid down and I decided to get the unpleasant task over and done with. I fired my first shot into the head of the deer and was later told by experienced hunters that the first bullet would have done the job. However, muscle contractions caused the dead deer to move and in my ignorance I thought it was still alive, consequently I fired two more shots to ensure that the animal was not suffering.

Back on the highway Constable Norman was waiting with the driver who had struck the deer. When they heard my third shot she shouted at him, "What's he doing in there?" to which the Constable replied "I don't know but I am not going to look, it sounds like the deer is shooting back!"

At this point I walked out of the bush with the deer's blood splattered over my shirt to be greeted by the woman screaming "Murderer" at me. I reminded her that I had not driven into the deer and was merely cleaning up someone else's mess!

On my return to the office I asked Sergeant Ted Scott, the supervising officer on duty, for three replacement bullets. Scott was an avid hunter and an excellent marksman who had earned the nickname, "One Shot Scott."

As I explained how I had needed three bullets to dispatch a deer with a broken leg, he gave me a withering look as he probably wondered about the quality of the recruits who were being hired.

Several weeks later I was working the night shift in the Horseshoe Bay area and came across an injured cat on the Squamish Highway. A car had struck it and the rear part of its body had been completely crushed. The cat was still alive and I ended its suffering with two bullets. Despite what the hunters told me, I could not be sure it was dead with the first bullet when its body went into convulsions. I radioed the police station and told the dispatcher that if they received any calls about "shots" fired on Highway 99 it was me just killing an injured cat. Within seconds Sgt. Scott's voice came on the air and in an incredulous tone questioned how many bullets I had used to kill a cat?

I later sheepishly returned to the office to get my replacement bullets and had difficulty looking the sergeant in the eye.

During the next 28 years of my career, I occasionally had to draw my gun but never had to fire it again except on target ranges, much to the relief of injured animals in West Vancouver.

Police Shootings

I RECENTLY READ A posting on Facebook where the writer thought that the police were too trigger happy. The story referred to an incident where a woman wielding a knife was shot by police. The writer wondered why the police "couldn't carry a net" and subdue threatening suspects by throwing the net over them! While it may have worked for the Roman Gladiators it is not a practical solution to dealing with suspects who pose a deadly threat to police officers and members of the public.

The police face many dangers in their daily duties and are obliged to follow many rules and guidelines when dealing with potentially dangerous people. But at the end of the day they have a responsibility to return home to their families in one piece. Despite many stories of police using excessive force while making arrests, the truth is that police officers, on a daily basis, risk their lives to keep society safe. When the police do kill someone, you can rest assured that the officers involved will be second guessed by the media, senior officers and politicians. They will be spotlighted in the media for months and perhaps years. However, when a police officer faced with a dangerous situation "gets it right" and defuses a potentially dangerous situation without anyone getting hurt – that will result in a passing mention in the media and be forgotten very quickly.

Corporal Dick Clancy of the West Vancouver Police was faced with a potentially explosive situation – this is how he dealt with it, in his own words.

"It all started as a routine day at the office. I was responsible for policing the Capilano Indian Reserve and I had been trying to arrange a sit down meeting with my North Vancouver RCMP counterpart, so we could discuss native policing issues. We finally settled on 5p.m. September 23rd 1994. That turned out to be a remarkable day and there were many twists of fate that came into play. We had agreed to meet at the White Spot Restaurant in the Park Royal Shopping Centre.

When I arrived I told dispatch that I would be turning off my radio, so we could have an uninterrupted conversation. I advised them that they could reach me on my cell phone if I was needed. As we were seated in the restaurant having our discussion, the other officer's pager went off, she needed to make a telephone call. I offered her my cell phone which she used to place her call – cell phones in those days did not have call alert. Unbeknownst to both of us, my office was trying to call me at that exact time. The call centre had been flooded with calls concerning a deranged male, dressed in army fatigues, who was stalking people with a rifle in the area of the Capilano River – very close to where we were. Dispatch was unable to reach me because my cell phone was in use. Had they reached me I would have left the restaurant immediately to search for him by the Capilano River and would most likely have not seen him approaching the restaurant through the busy shopping mall parking lot!

We finished our meeting at 6 p.m. and as we left I noticed the restaurant was very full, with approximately 50 people waiting in the lobby to be seated. There was a long line of people waiting to pay their bills so I told my RCMP counterpart that I would look after our bill and she left. An elderly man in front of me turned around and said I probably had more important things to do that he did and told me to go ahead. This played a critical part in the timing of what was about to take place. I paid our bill and made my way to my unmarked police car which was parked at the eastside of the restaurant. The communications centre was flooded with calls and did not try to contact me again – I had no way of knowing about the imminent danger.

I got into the car and started the engine and as was my habit, I put the driver's window down a few inches. As I began to pull ahead I heard the distinctive sound of a rifle action being worked. I looked to my left and there walking within ten feet of me was a male dressed in full army battle dress. He had a huge backpack on his back, his face was painted with camouflage paint. He was sweating so profusely that the drops were raining off his face. He racked another round through the chamber of the bolt action weapon he was carrying. He was so close that I could easily see that he had live ammunition. He pushed the two rounds he had into the clip through the breech of the weapon, he then racked a live round into the chamber as he walked around the corner of the building, heading towards the entrance of the restaurant.

I quickly put my car in park and left the vehicle, as I did I put my portable radio on my belt. I rounded the corner of the building and saw the suspect walking at a normal pace towards the entrance to the restaurant. I knew I had to take immediate action and I actually considered shooting the man to prevent him from harming others. The problem was his large backpack covered all but about two inches of his head. The other issue was because of the angle we were at, my backdrop if I missed, was the open front door of the restaurant which I knew had a packed lobby. The man was much larger than I was but I made the instant decision to attack him from behind, face plant him onto the pavement and take control of him in what I knew would be a violent desperate struggle.

I started towards him and suddenly the portable radio on my belt came to life, broadcasting "all units, the deranged male with a rifle has been sighted in Park Royal South by a Blue Bus driver." The man heard it at the same time as me and he spun around. I quickly keyed the mike on my radio and gave my call number, the police code for officer in distress and my location. I then turned my radio off – I knew my fellow officers would be responding and I didn't want the suspect to have the tactical advantage of being able to hear their radio transmissions. I did not hold out much hope for my own survival at this point. The suspect began to very deliberately raise to the rifle to his shoulder. My mind was racing and time seemed to stand still. My first thought was that I wasn't going to get to go home tonight and I wasn't going to get to say goodbye to my children. Out of the corner of my eye I saw a man who was seated at a table by the window, reach across and drag a young boy out of his seat and across the table in an attempt to shield him. I knew I had to do something, my own death was imminent and I was not going to be able to protect our citizens who were sitting in the restaurant. If I dove to the left I would draw his fire towards the window – I was terribly outgunned, being armed with a .38 caliber revolver and him with a 30 caliber rifle. I thought if I dove to my right I would almost certainly be hit but there was a chance that my right hand would not be incapacitated and there was the possibility of getting one shot away. I didn't know if he was wearing a bulletproof vest and I still had the problem that my back drop, if I missed, was a lobby full of civilians. I heard female voices approaching from behind me and realized that drawing his fire would put them in peril. Incredibly those women actually brushed by me while I confronted the suspect and carried on into the restaurant, totally oblivious to what was transpiring right before them!

His rifle now had reached his shoulder height and I recall thinking, "this is it, it's over". I actually felt very calm as I saw the restaurant manager pulling the door closed and instinctively knew he was locking it.

I was later told by a police psychologist that what I did next was to throw myself into the suspect's world. I suddenly barked at him, in a voice that I had often heard on military parade squares. I said "Soldier, is your weapon loaded?" He barked back, "Yes Sir!" He began to look confused and very slowly began to lower his weapon. I thought my god that is the reaction I was hoping for. Which is strange in itself as I hadn't consciously formulated my actions as a plan.

I said, "Who is your commanding officer?" to which he responded that his commanding officer had been killed. I ordered him to "make safe" his weapon and he lowered his rifle and placed the butt on the ground while he held the barrel at his side. I kept asking him questions using military jargon and kept him talking while I slowly approached him. When I got to him I ordered him, in military fashion, to surrender his weapon. He allowed me to take it from him. I opened the breech and placed the weapon on the ground. I considered throwing the rifle onto the roof of the restaurant but reasoned that this may trigger a physical confrontation.

The danger was not over, he had a large knife in a sheath across his chest and there was something taped to his left upper arm. He kept reaching towards that object and I kept knocking his hand aside. I was concerned that it may have been a grenade. He had numerous pockets and his pack that could conceal weapons – I was concerned *that he was going to blow us to "Kingdom Come". I heard sirens coming and decided not to try and search him without assistance. I turned on my radio and heard the familiar voice of Cst. Colin Bursill, "I've found his car, it is running and the door is open in the east parking lot". Out of my sight, Cst. Bursill had peeked around the corner and saw I was engaging the suspect. Bursill then ran around the building and he suddenly appeared behind the suspect, grabbed him from behind by the elbows. I removed the knife from him and searched his pockets, I did not find any more weapons. The suspect was in possession of several speedy loader clips and had a total of 57 live rounds of ammunition in his possession.*

Other officers arrived and took charge of the suspect. He was totally delusional and while being transported to the hospital, he told Cst. Rick Catlin that he had died from lung cancer and had gone to heaven. God had introduced him to a beautiful woman who he had married before Jesus Christ. God had told him three days earlier that he had to prepare for a mission back on earth – he was to stop taking his medication and he was to meet God at the White Spot restaurant at 6 p.m. on Friday!

A later search of his apartment revealed two semi-automatic handguns with several fully loaded clips laid out beside them. It is believed that he was preparing to go back to his apartment to fend off a siege.

I got to go home that night and I told my children that I loved them! The suspect was eventually released back into the community following psychiatric treatment.

Often time working in a police car you feel alone and isolated and you often wonder if you are making a difference. After this incident was reported in the press I received a very touching letter from a young lady whose life I had saved the previous year. She gave me all the reassurance that I needed to know that I was indeed making a difference and I am also grateful that I did not need to use deadly force to stop the suspect.

I was awarded the Distinguished Police Service Medal for valour as a result of my actions in this incident. To my knowledge I am the only serving or retired member who ever received two medals for valour. To this day I am in possession of the "bullet that had my name on it!"

Cpl. Dick Clancy.

Detecting 101

WHILE TODAY THERE are many training courses that develop the skills of a detective, it is still necessary to develop the basics through good old fashioned police work. The type of work that is learned in the early days while working in uniform out on the street.

When I was first promoted to the rank of detective, I was lucky to have Staff Sergeant Jack Ross as the man in charge of the Criminal Investigation Division (CID). I had first worked with Jack Ross when I was a rookie constable and many of the skills I had developed in uniform, that gave me the basics to be a detective, were learned from him.

In the world of fiction, it seems that police officers can knock doors down with one swift kick. Kicking in doors is an art that can be fraught with dangers and surprises! In my very early days as a constable in uniform, I was taken along on a "drug raid". The main party would hit the front door and I was sent, with another officer, to come in through the back door. These raids were known as "no knock warrants" because if you announced your presence, the evidence was likely to be flushed down the toilet before you got inside. The Sgt. gave the signal over the radio once we were all in position. The more senior officer that I was with, was built like a tank and he charged the back door – only to bounce off it like a tennis ball. Not to be deterred, he took another run at it with the same results. This man was not the sharpest knife in the drawer, and he braced himself for another run just when the Sgt. poked his head out of a window and suggested that we come through the front door. He then led us to the back door and grinned as he pointed to it – it had been bricked up!

Shortly before my move to CID I had another "learning experience" with kicking in doors. A distraught man called the police station to report that his former girlfriend was attempting to take her own life. She had not accepted their breakup and had a history of attempted suicide. She had called him at his office and told him that she was taking an overdose of drugs, as he spoke with her he noticed that her speech was starting to slur. While he tried to keep her talking he called the police on another telephone and I was dispatched to her address, in a high rise apartment. The apartments were all owned by the residents. Consequently, there was no manager with a pass key, however, I managed to get into the building but could not access the woman's home. She did not respond to my knocks on the door and I was told, via radio, that she was no longer responding to her former lovers' voice on the telephone. The other emergency services had not yet arrived so I decided to kick the door in. I stepped back into the hallway and with my right foot upraised, I launched myself at the door. To my utter amazement the door, complete with door frame, fell into the apartment. Wow! I thought, I don't know my own strength. I proudly strode over the collapsed door and found the women in her bedroom. At this point Fire and ambulance arrived and took over care of the suicidal woman. Thankfully, she later fully recovered.

However, I was about to have my oversized ego deflated. Constable Peter Norman had arrived to see if he could help. As I described my devastating kick, he beckoned me over to the door frame and pointed to some nails. They had been called to the home the previous day for a similar call and taken the door and frame down with a sledge hammer. Peter had just "tacked" the door back into place with a couple of nails, as a temporary measure, until the door and frame could be properly fixed.

My next humiliation was also witnessed by Constable Norman! As a new detective, I was working the afternoon shift by myself. Patrol passed along a fraud case in which it appeared that the suspect had left his name and address, which was in the City of Vancouver. While I was under no illusion that I would find the suspect at the address, there was the possibility he was known by someone there and I might be able to trace him. Rather than call the Vancouver Police for assistance, I checked with the duty sergeant to see if he could spare one of his patrol members. An hour or so later Peter Norman had changed into his civilian clothes and we drove to the address. As we entered the building we realized it was some sort of care home for the elderly. A uniformed nurse was sitting behind her desk. As we approached I began identifying ourselves and flashed open my wallet in a sweeping movement, to show her my police badge. This resulted in all my credit cards, drivers' licence etc. flying out of my wallet and spreading themselves far and wide across the floor! As I crawled around on my hands and knees picking everything up, Constable Norman explained the reason for our visit. She knew the person we were looking for and described him as an 80 year old man whose wallet and identification had been stolen. We quickly realized that our fraud artist was using this gentleman's identification. I tried to muster up a little dignity as I thanked the nurse and we quickly went on our way.

As we returned to West Vancouver we received a call on the police radio. The dispatcher asked if it had been us at the care home, the nurse had called and wanted to verify that we were actually police officers because of the "strange way we acted". The dispatcher had reassured the nurse that we were not allowed out alone, very often!

However, life in the detective office is not all fun and games and over the next number of years I was involved a wide variety of criminal investigations, some of which I would like to share with you. I will conclude this book with my biggest case, "The Motor Cycle Bandit". The bank robber had earned this moniker from his habit of stealing a motorcycle and then using it for his getaway after a series of bank robberies. When this man got bored with robbing banks he upped the ante by murdering a Brinks armoured car guard, Robert Persowich, and stealing the takings of a government liquor store in the Park Royal Shopping Centre, in West Vancouver. This resulted in my partner, Detective Colin McKay and I working with a team of investigators to bring this man to justice. But first I will share some other investigations with you. I hope you will find them interesting.

THE CLOSET DICKS

Left to Right: Leishman, Johnston, Fox, McKay, Schrierer. While we were unusually busy, when an officer recovered a box full of stolen clip-on earrings, we couldn't resist the chance to fool around for Cst. Andy Mendel's camera.

If the Shoe Fits!

In MARCH 1987, two men smashed their way into a West Vancouver house by breaking through a picture window using the butt of a shotgun. Both suspects were wearing surgical gloves and had covered their faces by pulling nylon stockings over their heads. After opening their safe at gun point, the terrified homeowners were tied-up and left to watch their "late evening visitors" empty the safe of its contents and disappear into the night. After freeing themselves and calling police, the robbery victims could only describe their assailants by approximate height and weight.

The patrol officers who initially responded to the call requested that Constable Andy Mendel, the department's identification officer, attend. Because the thieves had concealed their features behind stocking masks and had worn gloves to ensure that they would not leave fingerprints, the only evidence left at the scene was a partial footprint impression. Constable Mendel located this evidence on broken pieces of glass found at the point of entry. The shards of glass were subsequently assembled like a jigsaw puzzle and the impression photographed.

Left: A piece of glass with the suspect's footwear impression was found on a shard of glass located inside the residence near the point of entry. Right: Backlit footwear impression on a shard of glass.

It was now my job to identify who had worn the shoes that had left the footprint. While television detectives would have solved that in less than an hour, I am sad to relate that it took me several weeks. I circulated the circumstances of the crime to surrounding police forces and eventually got a call from an RCMP officer. To cut a long story short, the RCMP member identified two men who fit the Modus Operandi (MO) they were currently serving prison terms for robbery. However, following a check with the prison authorities, I learned that they had both been out of prison on the weekend of the robbery in West Vancouver. One had been on an unescorted-pass, the other was unlawfully at large after failing to return from an earlier day-pass. The suspect who remained in prison was the only hope of gathering additional evidence.

A surveillance team was assembled and assigned to follow the suspect on his next weekend-pass. He was subsequently given a 48 hour pass the following weekend. Towards the end of his first day out, he met with the second suspect who was still unlawfully at large. Both men were arrested as they left a restaurant in New Westminster. They were taken into custody for breaches of their temporary absence permits, however, at that time there was no solid evidence linking them to the robbery in West Vancouver.

Their shoes were seized and turned over to Constable Mendel for examination. The suspect who was unlawfully at large was found wearing a pair of "Nike" running shoes. Impressions from the right shoe matched the marks found on the glass at the crime scene. Raymond Spark was subsequently charged with robbery and wearing a disguise with intent. While I had no doubt the second suspect, Ralph, was involved in the robbery, there was insufficient evidence to lay charges against him and he was returned to prison authorities.

The only evidence against Spark was the shoe print impression. Constable Mendel's identification was positive, he found 11 points of comparison. The only potential problem was Spark might claim he had acquired the shoes after the robbery. With this in mind, a search for additional evidence was undertaken.

I remembered reading an article in the RCMP Gazette which I thought may be useful. It had been written by Sgt. J.R.G. Koehler of the Sydney, Nova Scotia RCMP Identification Section. The article entitled "Footwear Evidence" was dug out and proved to be of assistance. Sgt. Koehler described a process by which a suspect's foot was linked to a shoe found at a crime scene. This identification was done by examining a faint foot impression located on the insole of the found shoe. The impression was then compared and matched to the suspect's foot. A doctor of Podiatric Medicine subsequently gave evidence at Nova Scotia Supreme Court testifying that the suspect's foot had made the impression in the shoe found at the crime scene.

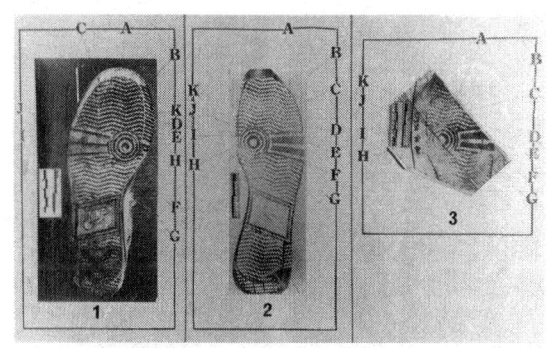

Comparison chart with Figure 1: the sole of the suspect's Nike running shoe. Figure 2: the test impression of the suspect's shoe. Figure 3: the actual footwear impression on the shard of glass found at the crime scene. Letters A-K indicate the accidental characteristics present.

While circumstances in the Nova Scotia case were different, certain similarities in this case warranted further exploration. The day before the preliminary hearing, I scoured Vancouver for a casting tray, a box containing pressure sensitive foam material. This was necessary to take an impression of the suspect's foot. With the manager of Hodgson's Orthotics Ltd. assistance, a casting tray and a quick lesson in its use was obtained. The next day the accused, Raymond Spark, was committed for trial based on Constable Mendel's evidence. He testified that the shoes worn by Spark at the time of his arrest were in fact the same shoes that had left marks at the crime scene. Following his committal, Spark was taken to the identification room where two impressions of his foot were taken using the casting tray. Constable Mendel later made plaster molds of these impressions. The foot was photographed and inked impressions were also taken. Following his return to prison Raymond Spark had been given a new pair of "Hawks" running shoes to replace the "Nikes" that had been seized at the time of his arrest. He had worn them for several weeks while awaiting his preliminary hearing. The "Hawks" were then seized as evidence as his feet had now left an impression in them.

The investigation to this point had been conducted with a copy of the RCMP Gazette held in one hand as a reference guide. The next stage was for Constable Mendel to photograph the insoles of both pairs of running shoes. This photography was done with the assistance of Ms. Annette Lythe, RCMP Crime Lab Photography Section, Vancouver. Earlier attempts at Reflective Infra-Red Photography had not produced the desired results, therefore, Ms. Lythe suggested Luminescent Infra-Red Photography. This proved successful.

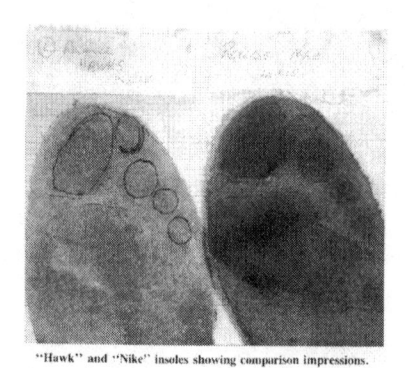

"Hawk" and "Nike" insoles showing comparison impressions.

Loaded down with plaster casts, photographs and inked impressions, Constable Mendel and I set out to find an expert witness who could interpret this evidence in court. After visiting a number of podiatrists, none of them had the expertise nor were willing to get involved in a potentially long court process. Eventually, Dr. Norman Gunn, a Toronto podiatrist, was contacted. Dr. Gunn gave evidence in the Nova Scotia case and was scheduled to give evidence at a preliminary hearing for a murder in Kamloops, British Columbia. Taking advantage of his presence in the province, he was asked to examine the exhibits.

After two days in West Vancouver, working with Constable Mendel, Dr. Gunn provided his report. While quite lengthy and detailed, the following paragraph extracted from his report clearly addressed police concerns. "There is no evidence that anyone else wore the "Nike" shoes other than the same person who wore the "Hawk" shoes and it is my opinion that the individual from whom the "Hawks" pair of footwear was taken is also the same individual who was the wearer of the "Nike" footwear."

At the subsequent trial in BC County Court before Judge Stuart Leggatt the testimony of both Constable Mendel and Dr. Gunn was accepted, despite a valiant attempt by the defence to discredit it. The defence lawyer later vigorously cross-examined me in an attempt to have the cast impression of his client's foot excluded as evidence. He claimed that his client's rights under the Charter had been violated by taking the impression without first advising the accused of his right to consult counsel. The judge eventually ruled in favour of the Crown and admitted the evidence.

All this preliminary work proved worthwhile. As suspected, Spark took the stand and stated that he had gone to a party several days after the date of the robbery. He testified that when he went to leave he discovered that someone else had taken his shoes. Spark went on to say that he left the party wearing the only unclaimed pair of shoes. You guessed it, they were the "Nike" shoes he was wearing at the time of his arrest!

Dr. Gunn's evidence went a long way to discredit Spark's contrived story. Without it, he would likely have been acquitted on a reasonable doubt. He was convicted on both counts.

Raymond Spark was sentenced to 8 ½ years in a federal prison for his part in the robbery. He planned to appeal his conviction and wanted to fund the appeal with his share of the loot. However, his partner in crime, now out of prison, was busy spending all the money. During a prison visit, Spark told his girlfriend, "I am going to speak to Leishman". He had obviously decided to "roll over" on his partner in crime. However, before he got the chance to contact me he was murdered in Kent Federal Prison on New Year's Day 1989, on the orders of Ralph, his accomplice!

Sgt. Stuart Leishman joined the West Vancouver Police Department in 1973. Following 8 years in the Patrol Division, he was promoted to Detective in the Criminal Investigation Division. With his promotion to Sgt., he has returned to patrol duties.

Sgt. Leishman has written and edited a book on child sexual abuse with over 20,000 copies distributed across Canada and abroad. He has a keen interest in police history and investigative techniques.

Cst. Andreas Mendel has been a member of the West Vancouver Police Department since 1979. In 1982, Cst. Mendel was assigned to the Identification Section and took the Identification Methods Techniques Course at the Canadian Police College that same year. In 1989, he attended the Senior Forensic Identification Course.

Cst. Mendel is a member of the Canadian Identification Society and was certified as a Senior Crime Scene Analyst by the International Association for Identification in 1990.

This article was submitted and accepted for publication in the R.C.M.P. Gazette.

The Mossad visits West Vancouver.

Mossad, short for HaMossad leModi in ule Tafkidim Meyuhadim is the national intelligence agency of Israel.

This legendary intelligence agency has many stories that would astound the world. It also has many agents, who eventually retire and take on roles in security and private investigations where they take advantage of the contacts they made during their active service to the State of Israel. One of these retired agents took on a job that eventually caught the attention of the West Vancouver Police Department.

A Dutch business man who lived in West Vancouver was a crook. He persuaded some European investors to put up money in a scheme he was promoting. As in many of these schemes, the business idea went bust leaving a lot of people out of pocket but somehow, leaving the Dutch business man much wealthier!

The investors tried the legal route and started court action but it became very obvious that the only people that were going to profit from that course of action were the lawyers, they decided to try a different approach! The Dutch business man was contacted by a mystery person who invited him to dinner at the Vancouver Delta Hotel at the Vancouver Airport. The unidentified man had a business proposition to make to him. Shortly after they sat down to dinner, the mystery man's cell phone rang and when he answered it he passed it to the Dutch business man. The person on the other end of the line said he represented the investors who had lost money on the scam and told the Dutch business man what was going to happen to him and his family, in very gruesome detail, if he failed to repay the lost money. He instructed the Dutchman to meet with his dinner companion the following day with the demanded funds in a suitcase. They agreed to meet at the same restaurant the next day.

The Dutch business man contacted the R.C.M.P, who policed the area and it was arranged that he would wear a wire and record the details of the meeting the following day.

When they met for dinner the following day an R.C.M.P.

surveillance team surrounded the hotel. However, as they set up they noticed a lot of retired R.C.M.P. members also set up in the hotel parking lot! The team leader moved in on one of the retired members and asked what they were doing there. To cut a long story short, the mystery man meeting with the Dutch business man was a retired Mossad agent who had worked in Canada and had hired the former Mounties to watch his back during a "business" deal. The retired Mounties were quickly sent on their way and the surveillance team moved in and arrested the retired Mossad agent once it became obvious that he was not going to say anything that would implicate him in a crime.

He was held in custody overnight but maintained he was an "innocent dupe". He claimed to have been hired to meet with the Dutch business man and then just pass the phone over to him when the call came in. He claimed to have no knowledge of the threats and stated he would never be a party to illegal activity!

The phone call was traced but it had originated in Israel and been linked through to a phone connection in Holland............ Nothing to see here folks!

Because the retired Mossad agent could not be linked to any crime in Canada, he was released and placed on a return flight to Holland. The Dutch business man returned to his home in West Vancouver and about 10 hours later received a telephone call from a pay phone that was later traced to Schiphol airport in Amsterdam. The caller said he wanted to thank him for the warm reception he had received in Canada and told him that the favour would be returned very shortly. Obviously, a not so thinly veiled threat. The business man contacted the R.C.M.P. who contacted the West Vancouver Police because the threat had been made in our jurisdiction.

I was the sergeant in the criminal investigation division and the case landed on my desk. It was obvious that we would not be able to prosecute anyone but I contacted the Dutch police authorities and they put the fear of god into the investors who had hired the retired Mossad agent. They consequently called off their former Mossad employees and resumed their legal attempts at restitution. I never did learn if they were successful in their efforts.

The One That Got Away – Almost!

IN THIS CASE *the man was never charged or convicted of any offence. I recommended charges but Crown felt there was not enough evidence to be sure of a conviction. I normally would not give his name but at the end of this story you will find a newspaper article that outlines similar circumstances involving the same man and at that time he had not been convicted, but was under investigation. I am relating the findings of my investigation and will leave you, the reader, to draw your own conclusion.*

On 03 September 1981, a man contacted the West Vancouver Police to report the theft of his car. Cst. Brian Hiebert took the complaint, which at the time seemed fairly routine. The man, Jaime, said that his 1963 Jaguar XKE, which he valued at $30,000 (1981 dollars), had been stolen from a parking lot in Horseshoe Bay, while he was visiting a friend on Vancouver Island. He also claimed that his suit, $500.00, and a pair of shoes, $300, had also been stolen with the car. He did not mention any of his identification or a wallet having being stolen and he said he still had the keys to the car.

On the 21st December 1983, the same man contacted the Richmond Detachment of the Royal Canadian Mounted Police and reported to Cst. Barry Edwards that his 1973 Citroen Maserati that he valued at $20,000 (1983 dollars) had been stolen. When he reported the theft to Cst. Edwards he was asked if there were any documents in the vehicle that would help the thief to personate him in order to sell the car. He replied, "No".

Later investigation would reveal that this man had an incredible run of bad luck. The following insurance claims had been made by him.

08 May 1981, he claims to have put his pencil case down while he was in Langara College bookshop. "It was stolen" and the insurance company paid out $1,139.60 for a gold pen, silver pen and other contents.

22 June 1981, he reported a break and enter at his house in Richmond and the insurance company paid him $9,146.19 for his

"stolen" stereo equipment.

30 August 1981, when he reported his Jaguar stolen in West Vancouver the insurance company paid him $1,075.00 for the suit and shoes he reported stolen with his car.

22 October 1981, he was paid $27,560.00 for his "stolen" Jaguar.

17 February 1984 he was paid $18,190.00 for his reportedly stolen Citroen Maserati.

03 October 1984, in keeping with his run of bad luck, he lost his wallet somewhere. It contained a MasterCard, a Bank of Commerce Visa card and two American Express cards, a Gold and a Green. Between the time he "lost" his wallet and reported them missing to the credit card companies, approximately $9,000.00 of cash advances had been made on these cards and the cash advances were within $100.00 of the credit limit he had on each card. In those days not all ATMs had cameras and coincidently, all the cash advances were made at machines without cameras!

In March of 1984 a car dealer in Vallejo California was considering buying a 1963 Jaguar XKE. He found service documents in the car that indicated it had been serviced by Coventry Motors in Vancouver. He called Coventry Motors who told him that the car had been reported stolen several years earlier. It was the same car that had been reported stolen to Cst. Brian Hiebert in West Vancouver. Word got back to the insurance company, consequently the situation was reported to The West Vancouver Police and I was assigned to investigate. I traced the Jaguar to ABC Motors in Vallejo, California. I contacted Officer Mike Gregory of the Vallejo Police Department and asked him to impound the vehicle until the investigation was complete.

This investigation can be likened to a bowl of spaghetti with strands leading from all directions. Shortly after I had been assigned to investigate the theft and subsequent recovery of the Jaguar, I was contacted by the Insurance Corporation of British Columbia and told of the reported theft and then finding of the Citroen Maserati in San Francisco, California, a short drive from where the Jaguar had been found.

Let's deal with the Jaguar first. Our unlucky citizen had reported that he left his Jaguar in a ferry parking lot on the 30 August 1981. He claimed to have been going to visit friends in Victoria on Vancouver Island but that when he got to the ferry terminal in Horseshoe Bay he found the electric fan, which formed part of the cooling system, was not working so he left the car there and went on the ferry as a foot passenger. When he returned from his visit, on 03 September 1981, he said his car was gone and he reported it stolen to Cst. Hiebert. He had the car key with him and claims there was only one key. He did not report any stolen identification.

The Jaguar was sold to R.S. Taylor Corp. (Classic Motors) in Vallejo California on the 02 September 1981 for US$7,000. The seller said he was Jaime, the registered owner of the Jaguar. He produced a Social Insurance card, a Bank of Montreal credit card and an instructional driver's licence, all in the name of the registered owner. He was given a cheque for the car which was cashed at a local bank using the identification mentioned above. The car had been sold and the cheque cashed, before the theft was reported to police. The buyer reported that the electric fan in the cooling system was in working order and that the car keys came with the vehicle.

During a later interview Jaime told me that he had gone to Vancouver Island to visit a friend who lived in Victoria. He was not able to explain why he had driven from his home in Richmond through a congested Vancouver, 35km over to the Horseshoe Bay Ferry Terminal which would take him to Nanaimo, 111 Km north of Victoria. When he could have driven from his home to the Tsawwassen Ferry Terminal, 22 km away which would take him almost into downtown Victoria. When I contacted his "friend" he told me he didn't know Jaime and he had just showed up on his doorstep saying he had got his address from a mutual friend, who at that time had moved to Switzerland.

The Citroen Maserati also had a complex set of circumstances surrounding its "theft". Jaime told the Richmond RCMP that he had left his vehicle at Mark's Import Auto Repair in Richmond for some service work. He said he left it there at 2pm on the 18 December 1983. He said he had forgotten to leave the car keys and had returned at 6pm and left them in a magnetic box under the bumper.

At noon the next day, a person who identified himself as Jaime, was at a car dealership in South San Francisco offering the vehicle for sale. The same person had been at another dealership, Forest Faulkner, earlier in the morning trying to sell the car.

Mr. John James of San Francisco was in the Citroen European Car dealership that day. He learned that a person who claimed to be Jaime was trying to sell the Citroen Maserati and eventually he made a private deal with the seller and bought the car. Later, Mr. James told me that the seller seemed fresh and rested and claimed to have been in San Francisco for several days. The seller said that his girlfriend had a brain tumour and was selling the car to raise funds to pay for surgery.

The seller had an intimate knowledge of the car. He described how he had converted the air conditioning system and showed Mr. James how to disconnect a wire under the hood which would shut off the air conditioning and improve the gas mileage. He also told the buyer that he worked on the floor of the Vancouver Stock Exchange. Jaime was a stock broker working for West Coast Securities.

On the 19 December 1983, Mr. James purchased the Citroen Maserati for US$10,000. He paid with a cheque that was made payable to Jaime. The cheque was cashed in a San Francisco bank using the follow pieces of identification, two credit cards and a temporary British Columbia drivers licence all in the name of Jaime. On the 21st December 1983, Jaime reported the theft of his car to Cst. Edwards of the Richmond RCMP. At that time he said there were no documents in the car that could be used to personate him. However, the next day he reported one of the credit cards, used to cash the cheque in San Francisco, stolen to his bank, but never to the police. None of the other pieces of identification were ever reported stolen or missing.

The insurance company paid Jaime $18,190.00 for the car on 17th February 1984. After he had received his cheque, Jaime called a Citroen dealer in Los Angeles and asked for a list of Citroen dealers in California. He later said he did this to try and find his car. He then telephoned Citroen European in San Francisco and spoke with Don Marriot at the dealership who told him that the vehicle was in their shop for repairs. He obtained a telephone number for Mr. James from them. He then called Mr. James and told him that the vehicle was his, he told Mr. James that "he would like to make a deal with him which would be to their mutual benefit. Mr. James later told me that his response was that the car was his and that Jaime would have to go through the courts to get it.

Jamie then contacted the San Francisco Police Department and spoke with Inspector Ted Peck of the SFPD. He claimed that his car had been stolen in British Columbia and that he had tracked it down to the Forest Faulkner dealership in San Francisco. Inspector Peck impounded the car until ownership could be determined.

So, I had two impounded car, the Jaguar in Vallejo and the Citroen Maserati in San Francisco. Both reported stolen by the same person and both allegedly sold by the thief in California. A thief who had an intimate knowledge of the vehicles and of the "owner" Jamie, the thief was also fully equipped with sufficient identification to satisfy the buyers that he was the legitimate owner of the car, and good enough that two banks in California would cash the cheques for him. My suspicious mind told me that something was wrong here!

After gathering all the details I arranged to interview Jaime. He was reluctant to meet with me, claiming to be a very busy person. However, after telling him I would just come to his place of work, he agreed to meet with me. During the interview he was very vague with me and just read through some papers from his briefcase, avoiding any direct eye contact.

While doing some background investigation into Jaime I learned of his terrible string of bad luck, which proved to be very costly to a number of insurance companies.

It was my opinion that he was supplementing his income with a series of staged thefts where he arranged to sell his vehicles to buyers in the United States and after the cheques were cashed, he would report the thefts to police in Canada and make a claim on his insurance. However, my suspicions did not constitute evidence that would support a criminal case.

He established an alibi that showed he was in Canada when the vehicle were offered for sale in the U.S. Obviously he had an accomplice. During my background investigation I discovered an associate of Jaime who had a dubious background and fit the general description of the seller. I managed to obtain a search warrant for his house and while searching it I found a stereo system that matched the one reported stolen by Jaime from his house in 1981. Unfortunately, all serial numbers had been removed. I sent a "photo line-up" to the U.S. that included this individual. He was identified by both buyers of the "stolen" vehicles as looking like the seller, but neither one could make a positive identification.

I was not able to determine the exact time the Jaguar was "stolen" from Horseshoe Bay ferry terminal or the exact time it was offered for sale in Vallejo. However, I was able to pin Jamie down to the approximate time he had left his vehicle at Mark's Import Auto Repair in Richmond. I was also able to establish when the vehicle had been offered for sale in San Francisco the next day. My next step was to establish if the vehicle could have travelled from Richmond, British Columbia to South San Francisco in the time line that had been described. I contacted Citroen to determine the fuel capacity of this car and the approximate miles per gallon you expect to get. I also established the exact mileage from Richmond to the Forest Faulkner car dealership in San Francisco. I also obtained the weather and road conditions for that date, along the route that would have to be taken.

From what Jaime had said, the earliest time the car could have been stolen was 7pm on 18 December 1983. The car was offered for sale between 10am and 11am on the 19 December. So I had to examine the 15 to 16 hour time frame from when Jamie claimed to have last seen his car in Richmond, BC and when it was offered for sale in San Francisco 987 miles away.

I met with Dr. Frank Navin, of the University Of British Columbia Department Of Civil Engineering. Based on the information I had gathered, Dr. Navin completed a chart showing that under perfect conditions the earliest time that car could have arrived at the dealership where it was sold, was 10am on the 19th December 1983. However, Dr. Navin contacted Professor W. Homburger at the University of California, Berkley, at the Traffic Transportation Institute. Professor Homburger advised that during the morning rush hour that day there had been considerable traffic delays which would have made the arrival in San Francisco considerably later.

What this told me was that Jaime had lied about when he had left the car at the repair shop, it was a Sunday and there were no staff to corroborate when it was dropped off. He had obviously given the car to his accomplice much earlier in the day in order for it to be in San Francisco at the time it was sold.

Where did this get me? Nowhere! There was just not enough evidence to support criminal charges. However, Jaime did come to a sticky end. During my investigation I had uncovered other scams he was involved in. He took out a bank loan using an expensive car as collateral, he then bought a wreck of the same type of vehicle, took the serial number into the bank and told them he had sold the car they were using as security for his loan but that he had bought another and then gave them the serial number of the wreck. When he defaulted on the loan the bank found itself the owner of a hunk of twisted metal!

He also staged car accidents in order to make insurance claims and while I cannot say for sure, I believe that was his undoing. Several years after my investigation into him, Jamie was involved in a car accident in West Vancouver where the car flipped on its roof and he was left a quadriplegic.

However, being a quadriplegic did not slow Jaime down in his criminal life. He had a home designed for his handicapped lifestyle He claimed multiple grants and tax relief that he was not entitled to and eventually ended up in court charged with fraud.

Several years after I retired Joey Thompson, a reporter with the Vancouver Province Newspaper, did a series of articles on Jamie. She details his ongoing fraudulent lifestyle.

Detective Stuart Leishman waits for the iPad to be invented!

The Province Newspaper March 19 1999
Byline Joey Thompson

My phone call didn't make Jamie Coltart's day.

Nor will it please the Persons with Disabilities or Heritage Homes.

Nor the anti-poverty types or the Society of Plaque-providers

There'll be a stampede to dog pile me for picking on a hapless guy trapped in a wheelchair.

But even guys in with physical impairments have been known to fall from grace.

Not that Coltart has.

Documents just suggest it.

Paperwork on the desks of investigators employed by the Welfare Ministry and

ICBC, that is.

True, these government bureaus don't top the popularity polls. And they know it.

Which explains why officials were twitching when it came time to release the goods

On their most recent fraud suspect – a quadriplegic who they allege took taxpayers and motorists for nearly a quarter of a million dollars. A wheelchair-bound heritage buff who recently scooped a North Vancouver appreciation award for investing three years and mega thousands decking out his home.

It's not politically correct, they murmured, delicacy is required.

Given it seems impossible to pry a nickel from ICBC for a claim that's legit, it's hard to imagine receiving money for one that isn't.

But 80 people were charged with 137 fraud related charges last year, and the courts found 56 of them (nearly two thirds) guilty.

Indeed, the activities of insurance scammers add about $150 to each annual auto plan premium.

Up to 15% of Canadian insurance claims are cooked, the Insurance Bureau of Canada estimates – costing us a tidy $2.3 billion a year.

Vancouver warrant No.98-549, court file No. 33946, police file No. 99-7705N1 dated a week ago set out the reasons why police collared Coltart, former VSE stockbroker, on three counts of criminal fraud over $5,000.

Perhaps the 6,200 square foot heritage home Coltart's just finished restoring was financed by the million dollar car injury cheque from the provincial government.

Then again, perhaps not.

It could be that your welfare taxes and insurance premiums bank rolled the replica renos, from 1910 light switches to old floor boards and rugs.

We'll leave that for Crown and the courts to decide.

What documents do show is that the welfare ministry started paying Coltart handicap benefits of roughly $1,000 a month in early 1993, shortly after he lost control of his Porsche on the Upper Levels Highway.

No question, he suffered permanent, debilitating injuries – his neck had snapped.

What they didn't know was that Coltart was also receiving $1,300 a month in wage loss benefits from the Insurance Corporation of BC.

The payment was based on a T4 slip he had submitted citing earnings of more than $100,000.

Police say it was closer to $7,000.

The warrant also claims Coltart failed to tell the ministry and ICBC about a pending $1.3 million settlement with the highways ministry and a road maintenance company.

Triple dipping?

For three years the charge sheets claim.

And then there is the matter of the souped-up Winnebago, a handicap friendly motor-home insured through ICBC for $95,000.

Stolen in June 1997, so the claim states.

After several months of no show, ICBC handed Coltart the cash and closed the file. Until a call came in from a trailer park near Merritt.

Something about a motor-home cramping space needed by vacationers in their stretch homes.

A licence plate check revealed a stolen vehicle.

"Stolen my ass," the trailer court manager is quoted as saying. "My son drove it here for the owner a year ago."

When contacted at his home yesterday, Coltart said he knew nothing about any charges against him.

"This is all news to me," he said, when I read from the charge sheet.

"I've not been served with anything. Besides, I was never aware of the welfare rules."

I had just had my neck broken and a social worker did most of the paperwork. This is going back over six years."

No trial date has yet been set.

My thanks to Joey Thompson and the Province Newspaper for their permission to reprint this story.

Eric Valois – A Well-Travelled Criminal.

AROUND THE WORLD IN 4,380 DAYS

The explosive story of an escape artist

By Stuart Leishman

A shoeless Eric Valois bolted to freedom in West Vancouver in 1986.

As you will see from looking at his mug shot, Eric Valois looks as if butter would not melt in his mouth. However, he was an extremely dangerous, resourceful young man who plied his criminal trade around the world.

My first dealings with Eric were in January 1986. He had travelled to West Vancouver from Montreal and had contacted distant relatives, looking for a place to stay while he looked for work. This family took him in while knowing very little about him. Sergeant John Looije was the Patrol Duty NCO on the 26th January 1986 and as a result of information he had received from a "source", Sergeant Looije obtained a search warrant for the house where Valois was staying.

I was called out, with another detective, to assist the Patrol members in the execution of this search warrant and to do the follow up investigation. The information that Sergeant Looije had received was that there was a suitcase containing a hand gun, blasting caps and dynamite in the West Vancouver home. We evacuated the family from the house and learned from them that the suitcase belonged to Eric Valois, their distant family member guest. They told us he was out for the evening but expected him to return. When we searched the house we found the suitcase with its "explosive" contents in the bedroom that was being used by Valois.

We settled in to await his return to the house. One member was positioned outside on the street, to give us a "heads up" when the suspect was returning to the house. We turned out all the lights and locked the door to make it appear that the family had gone to bed. The home was a split level. From the entry hall by the front door there was a short staircase that led up to the bedrooms. I positioned myself at the top of the stairs with a patrol member and the other two police officers were positioned in the living room, just off the entry hall. We received a warning that someone was walking up to the front door, about 30 seconds later the door opened. We wanted him inside the house before we moved, a foot chase through the darkened and wet streets of West Vancouver did not appeal to any of us. Not to mention the fact that we had every reason to believe he was armed.

He closed the door and as he turned the lights on I launched myself through the air screaming like a banshee and landed on top of him. This had the desired effect and he crumpled into a defensive ball, before he knew what was happening he was securely handcuffed and being read his Charter of Rights.

Our dealings with Eric Valois were going to be very limited at this point. I intended to conduct a thorough investigation into the source of the blasting caps, dynamite and the handgun. I also wanted to know what he planned to do with them. However, Eric had different plans and they did not include establishing a long term relationship with the West Vancouver Police.

On the night of his arrest I conducted a brief interview with him in the cell block interview room. His response to questions about the hand gun and the sticks of dynamite were essentially that he had transported them to the West Coast from Montreal for someone else. He claimed that he was to be paid a few thousand dollars for doing the job. Beyond that he was not prepared to say anything more and asked for a lawyer. We had also found hypodermics in his suitcase along with an envelope containing white crystals, they later analysed to be heroin and the fresh needle tracks on his arm confirmed that he was a heroin addict.

I spent several hours preparing a report for Crown Counsel so that we could bring him into court the following morning. Then, home for a few hours' sleep.

When we arrested Eric Valois he was a parolee from the Federal Prison System. He had been serving time for: Eleven Counts of armed robbery, possession of a prohibited weapon, escape lawful custody, conspiracy to commit an indictable offence and being disguised with intent to commit an offence. Eric was serious criminal material!

The next day I spoke to the Provincial Sherriff who brought the prisoners into the court room from the cells for their appearance before a judge. I told him that this man was an escape risk, he had an extensive record for escaping from police custody, and under no circumstances was he to be brought into court until I was also in the courtroom. I then began doing some background investigation into Eric, and the possible source of the dynamite. I spoke on the telephone with his grandfather in Montreal. He told me that Eric had been staying with him before his trip to the west coast and that he had left a large trunk at his house. I asked him to look in the trunk and when he came back on the line he stammered that the trunk was packed with dynamite! I told him to hang up the phone and call 911 and then to leave the house until the authorities arrived. I then called the Montreal police to advise them of the situation.

At this point my colleague, Detective Colin McKay burst through the door of the Detective Office to tell me that Eric Valois had just bolted from the courtroom, handcuffed and in his stocking feet, he was on the loose in West Vancouver!

Despite my warning that Valois was not to be brought into court unless a police officer was present, the Sherriff, afraid to keep a grumpy judge waiting, had brought him into the dock anyway. Only a few minutes into the hearing Eric Valois had vaulted out of the prisoners box and he then ran out of the fire exit onto the street. The area was cordoned off but it was if he had turned into mist – he completely vanished.

Despite the use of police dogs and keeping the area locked down for several hours Eric had taken his leave of West Vancouver hospitality and we would not meet again for many years, in fact until after I retired.

Before I tell you about the wondrous travels of our friend, I will share the source of the dynamite and the hand gun with you. Eric Valois had broken into the explosives shed at a mine in northern Quebec and the trunk load of high explosives and blasting caps found in his grandfather's house in Montreal had come from that. The loaded .38 calibre Smith and Wesson hand gun that we had found in his possession came from an armed robbery he committed in Quebec, he had taken it from a security guard while he was robbing a bank.

Later in the evening of the day that Valois escaped, we learned that he had broken into a house in the 1300 block of Duchess Avenue, a block away from the police station and had laid low for the day. Once the road blocks had been taken down, he stole clothing and credit cards from Mr. Paul Valastin, the man whose home he had broken into. This break and enter was not discovered until the home owner had returned home from work that evening. Valois then made his way to Horseshoe Bay and caught a ferry to Vancouver Island. He made his way to Sidney, a small community south of Victoria and there he stole a boat from a marina.

Our next contact with Eric Valois was when we received a call from the King County Sheriff's Department in Washington State in the United States. We learned that our fugitive had sailed the stolen boat into Lake Washington and tied it up at a marina. He had met a young woman who he took out for drinks and when she drove him back to the Marina they discovered "his" boat was missing. The boat had in fact been seized by the King County Sherriff's when they discovered it had been stolen from Vancouver Island. She said she told him he should report it and he seemed reluctant, I wonder why? She dropped him off at the police station in Seattle and never saw him again. The King County authorities found the fingerprints of Eric Valois in the stolen boat along with some credit cards slips from Mr. Valastin's stolen credit card. At this point the trail went cold.

I did not hear anything about Eric Valois until July 1986, seven months after he had escaped from West Vancouver. He was arrested for shoplifting in Reno Nevada. He was held in custody and when he appeared in court the following day he pled guilty to theft and was sentenced to seven days in goal. The day after his release, authorities at the shopping mall where he had been arrested called police about an abandoned van that had been in their parking lot for a week. The attending police officer found that the van had been stolen in California and that it contained a sawn off shotgun, wigs and an incendiary device, a police scanner along with other disguises. This vehicle was linked by fingerprints to, no prizes for guessing, Eric Valois. When he had been arrested he was fingerprinted but a search of the national files had not been completed before his release. This is probably what he was banking on with his swift guilty plea.

The following month, August 1986, our fleet footed criminal was arrested again, this time in the Bahamas. He had stolen a 65 foot yacht, valued at $450,000 (1986 dollars) from a marina in West Palm Beach in Florida. He sailed it to the Bahamas but it was his misfortune that a friend of the yachts owner was also in the same marina and knew it did not belong to Valois. They called the police and our friend was now back in custody. When Valois was been flown back to Florida he was transported in a light aircraft and as the plane taxied along the runway, he tried to make a break for it by attempting to jump out of the open door. However, he was overpowered. He was taken into custody by Detective Jack Yates of the West Palm Beach city police.

Now this is where the story becomes completely bizarre and Eric Valois is aided in his next escape by non-other than the Quebec Provincial Police, who thought he was their ticket to solving the Air India bombing case – a terrorist act that saw an Air India aircraft blown out of the skies as it passed by the Irish coast.

Detective Jack Yates of West Palm Beach City Police was preparing charges surrounding the theft of the yacht. He was also in touch with the police in Reno, Nevada who held warrants for him. Special Agent Jim Cavanaugh of the Federal Bureau of Investigation also filed charges against Eric Valois of Interstate Transportation of Stolen Property.

In West Vancouver we were contacted by Interpol Canada and told about the arrest of Valois in Florida and of the charges he faced in the U.S. At the time we held a Canada Wide warrant for his arrest on the West Vancouver charges. Eric Valois was a popular guy, who was wanted by many police agencies across North America.

My supervisor, Staff Sergeant Ed Pruner, was contacted by the FBI and asked how badly we wanted Valois. S/Sgt Pruner told him that we wanted him here to face charges but if he faced charges in the United States, we were content to wait until he had served his time there. That was the last official communication we had regarding Eric Valois. We imagined he would be serving a lengthy prison term in the U.S. before we saw him again. This was in September 1986.

Several months later a colleague in the Royal Canadian Mounted Police contacted me and said he thought Valois was back in Canada and being held by the Quebec Provincial Police. Attempts to verify this were met with a wall of silence. In March 1987, Corporal Laurie MacDonnell of the R.C.M.P. advised me that the Q.P.P. had confirmed they were holding Valois without charge on the 4th floor of a detention centre attached to the Q.P.P headquarters. Cpl MacDonnell flew to Montreal to interview Valois in connection with one of their cases. I met with Cpl MacDonnell on his return to British Columbia and he confirmed that the Q.P.P. were in fact holding Valois but it was not clear to him under what circumstances or authority that the Q.P.P. was holding him.

While in Quebec, Cpl. MacDonnell pointed out that the West Vancouver Police held a Canada Wide Warrant for the arrest of Eric Valois but the Q.P.P. responded that those charges would probably be waived to Quebec for a guilty plea.

THE PLOT THICKENS! On the 13th April 1987, I received a call from Cpl. MacDonnell, he told me that Valois was no longer in custody! His information, from an "unofficial source" was that Eric Valois had been released, unsupervised, to visit his sister! He failed to return. As the French would say, "Quelle Surprise!" On the 14th April 1987 Eric Valois was entered on CPIC (Canadian Police Information Computer) as unlawfully at large by the Quebec Provincial Police.

Any attempts to get an explanation from the QPP were fruitless. I would have to look elsewhere for answers.

Following telephone conversations with police officers in the United States and further information I received from Cpl. MacDonnell, I managed to piece together the following narrative.

When Valois was arrested in the Bahamas and returned to Florida, Interpol notified the Canadian authorities of his arrest. Shortly after this, members of the Q.P.P. travelled to Florida and interviewed Eric Valois. They made some sort of deal with Valois and he agreed to waive all his rights to an extradition hearing. The Q.P.P. member then told Detective Jack Yates that they were representing all Canadian police forces. Later, Detective Yates told me that he thought he was dealing with the R.C.M.P., Canada's national police force. Andre Beauchamp was the police officer from the Q.P.P. He told Detective Yates and later Special Agent Jim Cavanaugh of the F.B.I. that Valois was responsible for eleven armed robberies in Canada. He also suggested he was responsible for the bombing of a shopping centre and they were led to believe that Eric Valois was implicated in the bombing of Air India flight 182. A Boeing 747 that was blown up by terrorists as it passed over the Irish coast on June 23rd 1985 with the loss of 329 lives.

Faced with this "story" the U.S. authorities agreed to withdraw their charges and let Valois be returned to Canada with the Q.P.P. members.

The Q.P.P. brought Valois back to Canada and because he was a Federal Parolee he was committed to a Federal prison to continue serving his sentence. Very soon afterwards Eric Valois was moved from the Federal prison and then held at the Q.P.P. "Centre of Prevention" a holding facility attached to the Q.P.P. Headquarters.

While I never received an official explanation of what had transpired, from speaking with a variety of sources I think that the Q.P.P. thought they had a link to the Air India bombing and decided to solve the case themselves without involving the R.C.M.P. task force that was investigating this horrendous terrorist act.

Eric Valois was happy to string them along as it had rescued him from a lengthy prison term in the United States and he was living a great life at the Q.P.P. detention centre. He was frequently allowed to leave, unescorted, to tend to his banking and other personal needs. I don't know if Valois thought the "jig" was up or if the Q.P.P. realized that they had been taken for a ride and decided he was too big of an embarrassment to keep around – but for whatever reason, Valois was allowed out for one last unescorted release from which he never returned!

You might think that you have heard the last of Eric Valois, if so you are mistaken. Several years later I was contacted by Interpol. Eric Valois had been arrested in Greece, he was in possession of an expensive yacht that had been stolen in France. This is the message I received from Interpol. *"We have been advised that Valois, while being escorted by the Athens Security Police to the Island of Rhodes to stand trial, jumped off the ship Kamiros. The escape occurred on 28th March 1988 at 06.15hrs near the Island of Tilos. Police confirm that one life ring is missing. Valois asked to go to the washroom and had his handcuffs removed by the guards. He entered the washroom and apparently jumped overboard. An air and sea search proved to be unsuccessful. To date neither Valois nor his remains have been found!"* I shed an inquisitor's tear for Eric, I was going to miss his travelogue.

A number of years passed, I was promoted to Sergeant and eventually took early retirement due to health reasons. However, Eric Valois was to cross my path once more. Several years into my retirement I was contacted and told that Eric had surfaced, so to speak, in Leeds, a city in the north of England. He had been arrested for drug trafficking. Since my retirement, files had gone missing and exhibits had been destroyed because the people in charge of those things assumed he was dead. At the end of the day he was successfully extradited and was returned to face his charges in West Vancouver. I still had my notebooks and I always kept copies of my reports so we went to trial in the Vancouver courts where he was successfully prosecuted by an excellent prosecutor, Ms. Ellen Gerber. He received a prison term - but I am not sure how long they would have been able to hang on to him!

Police and the Mentally ill.

During my career as a police officer I had many dealings with the mentally ill. Some years ago society in many western countries decided to close down mental institutions. The thinking was that with the advent of so many new drugs, people could be treated outside of an institutional setting. While the reasons for this change in approach to treating the mentally ill, would in many instances, be a more humane way to treat people, the infrastructure that was needed to support them was not put in place.

Men and women were turned loose on the streets and without the necessary support, many quickly fell into substance abuse and became the "homeless" that are so prevalent in major cities today. For many years the police and courts have been left to deal with the resulting chaos on the street. What follows is a story of one of the dealings that I had with a mentally ill person.

Leonard had stabbed a West Vancouver bus driver over a fare dispute. Luckily the driver was not seriously injured and Leonard was taken into custody by the West Vancouver Police, who held him for a court appearance. When Leonard was lodged in the cells a search of his back pack revealed some rather disturbing pornography. The magazines featured breast binding and a variety of torture involving women.

As it was a Saturday I was the lone detective on duty so when I was presented with this material by the patrol division I felt it warranted an interview with Leonard. We spoke at length and what I thought would be a short interview turned into a six hour marathon. Leonard had suffered from mental illness most of his life and spent many years in institutions. His condition was controllable with medication and once he was stabilized he was turned out on the streets with a supply of pills. The drugs controlled his mental issues but then he was feeling fine and decided that he no longer needed them! He would get into trouble be arrested and returned to a hospital setting where he would be stabilized and returned to the streets where the whole cycle would begin again.

I spoke to Leonard about his magazines and he told me about his desires to torture women. He described living in Edmonton and frequenting a trail which female students would use, he spent many hours lurking in the bushes waiting for a victim but other people passing by at the same time prevented him from attacking them. He spoke about becoming fascinated by an exotic dancer in a Vancouver bar. One day he followed her home, a basement suite. Once he had established where she lived Leonard went to the house the next day while she was at work. He broke into the suite and set about planning his attack on her. He hid in a closet and waited for her to return home. As he whiled away the time in the closet, he noticed a light and thought that the switch was on the outside. Leonard explained that while he had exotic plans in mind for torturing this young lady, he would have been embarrassed if, she had turned on the closet light before opening the door, and seen him.

Leonard was carrying a knife to use on his victim and decided to cut the light cord. What he did not realize was that the light control was at the bulb and that he was cutting into a live electrical line. His cutting action resulted in a large flash and a loud bang. The landlord lived upstairs and came to investigate the noise. He confronted Leonard who claimed to be a friend of the young woman. The landlord made him leave the house and then called the police. Leonard was arrested but due to his history of mental illness he was just returned to the mental institution where the whole cycle would be repeated. Before Leonard appeared in court the next week, I gave the prosecutor an extensive report detailing my findings and stressing the need to have him detained for a psychiatric evaluation. However, while Leonard had psychiatric problems, he was not stupid. Through his legal aid lawyer he was willing to plead guilty to the assault on the bus driver and spend seven days in jail rather than submit to an evaluation that he knew would return him to an institution.

Despite my protests, Crown Counsel took the guilty plea, it was the easy way out!

I tried to keep track of Leonard over the next few years but he disappeared into the woodwork. I could only hope that his bumbling attempts to become a sadistic murderer would continue to fail.

All this happened in the 1980s and what brought it to mind was the attack on Cpl. Nathan Cirillo at the Canadian National War Memorial in Ottawa, the nation's capital in 2014, by Michael Zehaf Bibeau and the murder committed by Brian Whitlock of his mother in Vancouver at around the same time. Both these men had a long history of mental illness and had been involved in the criminal justice system. If the courts were not cursed by incompetent prosecutors or laissez-faire Judges perhaps these men would have received the treatment they needed and their victims would not have become VICTIMS!

Gerry, a Sandwich Short of a Picnic!

GERRY WAS A classical bully, a thug who thought he could get what he wanted in life by intimidating people. Whenever he was stopped by police for his frequent driving infractions he would leap out of his car and begin screaming and threatening the bewildered police officer who had stopped him. This happened so often that he and his vehicle were listed on CPIC, the police computer as being a "Code 5 check", potentially dangerous to police. I had a couple of run-ins with Gerry where he put on his best performances. In one instance when I was still in uniform, I stopped him and arrested him for failing to provide a breath sample, he had shown signs of impairment. Gerry made several threats that included finding me and my family, with a shotgun. Normally I would ignore that sort of drivel but because he specialized in trying to intimidate people, I also charged him with uttering threats. Several days later he telephoned me at the police station and began challenging me over the telephone. He said that he would like to take me on without my gun and suggested we meet in a parking lot to "duke it out". Of course I realized he was taping the telephone call and trying to goad me into saying something silly. I just very politely told him that his situation was before the courts and that he should speak with his legal counsel. At trial his lawyer suggested that I had said some improper things to his client, I of course denied this and in his best "Perry Mason" style he asked me what I would say if his client had a tape of this conversation! I replied that I would be delighted to listen to it. Of course there was no tape and Gerry was convicted.

Some years later when I was a detective, Gerry reared his head once more. His newspaper delivery boy was in the habit of throwing the rolled newspapers at the door in order to save himself a few steps. Gerry took exception to this and cuffed the young boys head. When the crying boy arrived home and told his parents, they called the police and made a complaint of assault. Gerry was arrested and charged with assault, which did not please him. He went to the boy's home and threatened the family. When the family realized they were dealing with a thug the father tried to withdraw the complaint. However, the police department were not about to withdraw charges because of intimidation, Gerry was warned to stay away from the family.

Sometime later a brick was thrown through the family's living room window and then shortly after that their van exploded in flames in their driveway. A police guard was posted on the family home and although we knew who was responsible for these crimes, there was no evidence to support a charge.

However, as previously mentioned, Gerry was a sandwich short of a picnic and he was about to supply police with the necessary evidence. He telephoned the father of the newspaper boy, who promptly turned on a tape recorder when he knew who was calling. He identified himself and said he would like the man to withdraw the charges against him. The father replied that he could not do that. Gerry then asked him if he had received his messages. The father said no, he had not received any messages from him. Gerry then went on to say that he had sent two messages over the past few days! The father pleaded ignorant of any messages and Gerry insisted that he had received them at his home. This was enough for Gerry to be arrested and charged with intimidating a witness. He was held in custody until his trial. Detective Brian Schierer was the investigating officer and it was my pleasure to accompany him when we went to Gerry's used car lot to arrest him.

At trial Gerry pled guilty to the charges. His lawyer said that Gerry regretted what had taken place and suggested that instead of a jail term, Gerry would be happy to rent a bus and take senior citizens to the upcoming Expo 86 that was to be held in Vancouver the following year. However, the judge made some comments about the safety of Vancouver's senior citizens and sentenced him to a term of imprisonment. Coincidently, I was at Expo 86 the next year, standing in line for the Australian Exposition when I found myself standing across from Gerry. I asked him if he had any seniors with him – he was not amused!

The Death of Grace Theodorou

THROUGHOUT MY CAREER as an investigator, both in uniform and as a Detective I had a great respect for the forensic investigators I worked with. The Identification Section of the West Vancouver Police Department was first developed by Gunther Wahl under the direction of the then Chief Constable, Moir MacBrayne. Gunther was a skilled photographer and this was the basis from which he built the "Identification Section" of the department. He worked with the Vancouver Police Laboratory to develop the fingerprinting techniques and other basic skills that the police department needed in those early days. Ted, (gloves) Johnston followed Gunther in the identification department. He was nick named "gloves" for his pronouncement that "They must have worn gloves" at any crime scene where he was not able to find fingerprints. George Philipson followed Ted Johnston and then Andy Mendel moved into the Identification Division and brought it to a whole new level of competence. New techniques were bringing forensic science to a much higher level than had been available in earlier days and Andy seized every new technique with gusto. We worked very closely together for many years and had some tremendous successes.

While the investigation into the murder of Grace Theodorou failed to gather sufficient evidence for a criminal charge it did illustrate some interesting forensic work on the part of Andy Mendel.

At the time of her death, May 1991, Grace Theodorou was a 21 year old female of mixed racial origin. Her mother is a Native Indian and her father is Greek. Grace had graduated from high school and she worked in her father's restaurant in Vancouver. She was in an abusive common law relationship with a 17 year old petty criminal, John, and she associated with a group of Iranian and Afghani males that frequented the skid row area of Vancouver. All these men were involved with heroin both as users and dealers. They were also known to pimp prostitutes. Grace was a heavy drinker, smoker, user of marijuana and had been known to try cocaine and heroin. She reportedly had an affair with an Afghani heroin dealer, Ahmed, while still living with John. All in all not a life style that pointed to a happy outcome.

Grace had last been seen in the early morning hours of 03 May 1991. From later interviews with her common law husband, John, it was learned that they had been out shopping at the Metrotown Shopping Centre in Burnaby, a suburb of Vancouver, on 02 May 1991. They had argued and he had driven off leaving her in the shopping centre. He said his next contact with her was when she paged him at 3 a.m. on the 03 May 1991. She asked him to pick her up at an apartment block giving him the address of 1330 Burrard Street in Vancouver, she did not give him a suite number. John said she sounded frightened and drunk, she said she was with two men, Faharani and Jelali. John asked her, *"Are they trying to fuck you?"* to which she replied, *"Yes!"*

John drove to 1330 Burrard Street but did not see her. He began ringing the buzzer of every apartment in an effort to locate her but was not successful and he was eventually escorted from the building by a security guard. This was later confirmed by the security guard. John paged her several times but never received a reply.

Later that day a beachcomber was walking on the beach at Ceperly Park in Vancouver, this is several blocks away from 1330 Burrard Street. He found a wallet that contained the identification of Grace Theodorou several feet from the waterline. Her identification was scattered within a 20 foot radius. He also found a stainless steel meat cleaver with a small piece nicked out of the blade. The beachcomber collected all these items and turned them in to the Vancouver Police. They entered the identification onto the National Police Computer System. Grace Theodorou was reported missing by her brother to the Vancouver Police on the 07 May 1991. The file was subsequently turned over to the Burnaby R.C.M.P. as Grace had resided in that community.

In the late afternoon of 05 October 1991 an elderly German tourist was picking mushrooms on Cypress Bowl Mountain in West Vancouver, approximately 40 kms from the beach where Grace's identification had been found. He found body parts and called the

West Vancouver Police. The investigators called in Andy Mendel, the Identification Officer. What he found at the scene was a dismembered body that would later be identified as the remains of Grace Theodorou. Her body had been hacked into pieces and placed in garbage bags before being dumped in the remote bush area on Cypress Mountain. Animals had torn the bags open and body parts had been spread around a ten acre area.

Corporal Mendel conducted an exhaustive search of the area, recovering all the body parts. This including seizing several heaps of bear excrement in which small bones belonging to the victim were found, one being a piece of vertebrae. Corporal Mendel had the bone fragments x-rayed and found a sliver of metal in the vertebrae recovered from the bear excrement.

The human remains were identified as being those of Grace Theodorou, from dental records. The identification and the cleaver that had been turned in to the Vancouver Police and then turned over to the Burnaby R.C.M.P. were now turned over to the West Vancouver Police who began a homicide investigation.

The Crime Laboratory made a comparison between the nicked blade of the cleaver and the sliver of metal found in the vertebrae. It was a perfect match. This cleaver had been used to dismember the body of Grace Theodorou.

When Grace was first reported missing the Burnaby R.C.M.P. conducted a significant investigation into her disappearance. They identified a number of people who had been in contact with the missing woman on the night she was last heard from. They included Nessam Jelali and Hassan Faharani, who was the resident of an apartment at 1330 Burrard Street. The last place that Grace Theodorou was heard from.

All the individuals who had information regarding the victim's movements on May 2nd/3rd 1991 were drug addicts, drug traffickers, prostitutes and pimps. Consequently the investigators had to sift through lies and misinformation to find some grains of truth. The basic story of that evening emerged as follows and appeared to have some credibility.

Following her fight with John, Grace went downtown and met

up with some skid row friends. Following a regular pattern, the group were drinking in several bars and ended up at the Balmoral hotel. Grace, Faharani, Jelali and a young woman called Cindy left the hotel in Faharani's car and drove around the downtown area and bought some cocaine. Faharani was drunk and driving in an erratic manner, this frightened Cindy and she demanded to be dropped off. They left her at Main and Hastings and drove off at approximately 2am. They may have gone to Jehali's apartment on Victoria Drive or to the apartment of Faharani which was at 1330 Burrard. It emerged that Jelali had a fascination for Grace and had tried to have sex with her, after getting her drunk several times, without success. It would seem that either Jelali or Faharani gave her drugs with the intent of having sex with her when she was unconscious. She died of a drug overdose and the pair panicked, disposing of her body in the bizarre manner in which it was found. Shortly after being questioned Faharni completely disappeared, it is believed he returned to Iran. Despite many hours of investigation it was impossible to establish the truth of what happened to Grace Theodorou and by whose hand she had died!

Death Has Many Faces.

As a police officer I had to deal with death in many forms – some stranger than others. As a young constable I received a call on the radio to attend a "routine sudden death". This in itself seemed strange but I assumed it was a natural death and that I just had to deal with the paperwork for the coroner. I went to the address given and expected to find an ambulance or the family doctor present. When I arrived no Doctor, ambulance or fire truck was evident so I knocked at the front door. An elderly man answered and invited me to come in. I asked him if the family doctor was here, "no", he said. Is the ambulance parked in the back lane I asked? "No" he said, "you are the first one!" I began to feel a little uneasy. I explained that I had received a call that there was sudden death at this address. "Oh yes," he replied, that is my wife, and she is in here. He led me through to the bedroom and a woman was lying in bed in a classic death pose, arms crossed on her chest. I quickly checked for a pulse and then held a mirror against her mouth in search for a sign of life. Finding nothing, I asked her husband what had happened. He explained that his wife had collapsed in the bathroom and that he had carried her to the bedroom, dressed her in a clean nightie and put her to bed. I asked why he had not called the doctor or an ambulance. He replied, "I did not know if she was dead yet!" At this point I became very uneasy and summoned an ambulance to verify that the lady in question had actually expired. At the end of the day the story that emerged was that the couple were members of a religion that did not believe in medical intervention. When his wife collapsed, he called members of his church and they all prayed. He did not call police until he was satisfied that she had died, it was a mutual agreement they both had. An autopsy showed that she had suffered a massive heart attack, the pathologist told me that even if she had been in a hospital she would not have survived so he was left in peace to bury his wife!

My other introduction to death involved a suicide. I received a call that a lady had arrived home to find her husband had committed suicide. I was barely out of the police academy and this was my first sudden death. I was given the address and was on my way with lights and siren blaring. I knew the street but not the number sequence. This street started at a junction and then circled around for a mile before coming back to the same junction. What I did not realize was that the home I was going to was two houses in from the junction. As I screamed past the junction the people at the house would have heard my approach and heard the siren die away before they heard it coming back again. It started out badly! When I arrived I was greeted by the dead man's wife and daughter. They showed me the spare bedroom where her husband was and he was obviously dead. I was stressed out and the extra mile drive had not helped. I rapidly thought back to my recent police academy days and remembered that instructors had told me that "hot sweet tea" helped people in shock. As I took them to the kitchen and tried to calm them, I quickly realized that they were quite calm and in fact were trying to calm me.

I later learned that the deceased had a long history of depression and his family were not surprised by his suicide. My later examination of the scene showed he had prepared for his death. He had left his Will and other important papers for his wife. He had laid on the bed and cut his wrists with a razor blade, which I found on the bedside table. It all seemed fairly straight forward but as it was my first sudden death I requested a Detective come to the scene. Detectives Hugh Carleton and Bob Willock came to the house and looked over the scene. I explained what I had done and they said that I seemed to have covered all the necessary steps and with that they took their leave.

The following day I received a call from the son of the deceased. He started out by thanking me for the way I had dealt with the investigation and his mother. Then almost as an aside, he asked me what I would like him to do with the "blood stained knife" he had found under the bed that his father had been on!

After I picked myself up from the floor, I told him I would come to the house right away. I then scurried down to the Detective Office to consult with Detectives Carleton and Willock. It seems that the dead man had tried to cut his wrists with a kitchen knife, without much success. He had thrown that under the bed and finished the job with the razor blade that I had found. The wise Detectives told me to thank the dead man's son, pick up the knife, place it in an envelope and quietly deposit it in the Exhibit locker! That was a valuable lesson in crime scene searching – I was much better at it after that experience!

Barricaded Suspects.

NEGOTIATING WITH BARRICADED suspects is a skill that has become highly developed over the last 40 years. The growing popularity of hijacking aircraft or taking hostages by terrorist groups in the 1960s and 1970s brought about a growing awareness that skilled negotiators were needed.

There was also recognition that special assault teams were required when negotiations broke down and an armed response was required. This became especially evident during the final showdown with the Symbionese Liberation Army (SLA) in Los Angeles on May 17th 1974.

The SLA had kidnapped newspaper heiress, Patty Hearst, and following a string of violent bank robberies, the bulk of the "army" was trapped in an East 54th Street hideout in Los Angeles. When word went out that the SLA were holed up in the house everyone who carried a badge and a gun in southern California decided to get in on the action!

Sometime later I attended a lecture given by an FBI agent who had witnessed the debacle. He related how more than 500 law enforcement officers from various agencies had shown up at the scene and during a two hour gun battle fired 9,000 rounds into the house. There was a complete lack of organization at the scene. No one was in overall command or knew what resources were on hand, let alone was able to direct a co-ordinated operation.

The purpose of the lecture was to encourage police agencies to develop negotiators and special armed response teams to deal with such events in a professional manner. In subsequent years much training has taken place and the province of British Columbia has many skilled negotiators and there are a number of competent armed response teams available to deal with any situation that may arise. This training also extends to the people who answer emergency telephones. If a call regarding a bomb or similar device is received the operator is trained to elicit as much detail as possible while listening to such things as background noises and accents.

However, the skills at our disposal today did not come easily or without their teething problems. The two incidents I am going to relate happened in West Vancouver but I have heard similar stories from colleagues around the country. Bomb threats were not an everyday occurrence in West Vancouver, but in the 1970s policies were developed to respond in a professional manner should we receive any. A checklist was kept by the telephone in the radio room of the police station that could be used in the event that a bomb threat was made. Several years after the shootout in Los Angeles that removed the SLA from the face of the earth, a West Vancouver dispatcher named Wilf received a telephone call. The caller claimed to represent the SLA and stated that a bomb had been planted in West Vancouver. Wilf was an excitable fellow and was not to be trifled with. He had experienced a particularly busy night and had many calls stacked waiting to be dispatched, as members became available. After the caller made his statement, Wilf replied, "Fuck off asshole, I'm too busy for that bullshit," And he hung up the telephone. While this is not a text book response, I am here to tell you that the SLA has never bothered the West Vancouver police since!

Barricaded suspects are another situation that requires special handling. When I listened to the FBI agent in the 1970s, he broke a barricaded suspect situation into three segments. The first stage he identified was containment, surround the location allowing no one in or out.

Stage two was negotiation where every effort was made to have the suspect release his hostages and surrender peacefully.

Stage three was an assault by an armed response team. This was usually triggered if a suspect began to kill his hostages.

The lecturer pointed out that if there were no hostages, it was his philosophy not to spend too much time on stage two and in the event of moving to stage three he "did not stress the carrying of handcuffs." I suspect when he retired he moved on to script writing for Clint Eastwood's "Dirty Harry" movies!

As a detective I was a trained hostage negotiator. However, I attended my first barricaded suspect situation as a junior constable while working in uniform. As I recall it was on the traditional "dark and stormy night" in fact it was raining cats and dogs. A family who lived in the wealthy neighborhood of the British Properties had reported that their son was locked in their home and they believed he had a gun. The boy suffered from depression and his intentions were not known. As one of the uniform constables at the scene my duty was containment. The two detectives on duty, Ron Denney and Bob Willock, would handle the negotiations. Several other uniform members and myself settled into positions around the house and tried to ignore the downpour while Denney tried to make contact with the barricaded suspect.

Bob Willock went to the house next door to see if he could see the young man from the neighbour's home which sat on higher ground. The suspect was not answering the telephone so Ron Denney tried to make contact with a bullhorn. At one point I heard Denney say on the police radio, "I bet it's dry up there Bob." To which Willock replied "yes, and the coffee is hot." As a young inexperienced constable I assumed that this was some sort of code for something. In actual fact Denney had seen Willock enjoying a hot cup of coffee brought to him by the resident, as he maintained his observation point in the neighbour's warm and dry living room. Denney was crouched in the pouring rain talking to himself through a bullhorn at this time.

Deputy Chief Constable Bob Brolly had come to the scene to see if he could be of help. He had arrived with another senior officer and after assessing the situation, he saw that there was nothing he could do and decided to return to the police station to get more rain gear for some of the men who had none. He asked Denney for the keys to his unmarked police car and promptly drove off. Halfway to the police station he ran out of gas. Detective Denney had grabbed the closest car when he left office and had not checked the fuel gauge. While miffed, Brolly picked up the microphone of the police radio and tried to contact the office. It was when he got no response that he looked at the radio set. The police radios we used at that time doubled as a portable radio. When they were lodged in the charger unit in the car they operated as a radio by using the attached microphone. However, the unit could be pulled out and used as a portable when the officer left the car. Brolly's radio was safely tucked into Denney's pocket, several miles away! It is hard to visualize how Brolly convinced some British Properties resident, whose home he went to, that he was in fact the Deputy Chief Constable of West Vancouver who had run out of gas and found he was without a police radio. However, Brolly was not called the "smiling Irishman" for nothing and he did convince them to let him in to use the telephone. I can report that his smile did disappear at the police station and words were later exchanged about empty gas tanks.

What about the barricaded suspect? He had been drinking and had fallen asleep. He later walked out to see what all the fuss was about and was arrested by a soggy Detective Denney

Drugs plus Sex plus a Contract Killer plus a Naïve Police Officer.

I AM INCLUDING THIS next story because of its unique set of circumstances. These incidents took place over 35 years ago but given the circumstances I will not be using any real names.

Staff Sergeant K had been a long term member of the R.C.M.P. and was approaching retirement. He had spent many of his later years as a policeman working in the drug squad and as retirement loomed he decided to supplement his pension plan by stealing some heroin from an exhibit locker. He approached Lulu, who he knew to be in the drug trade, to sell his ill-gotten goods. Lulu was delighted to do business with the crooked policeman and made a handsome profit in the process. However, the problem with doing business with a criminal is that there really is no honour among thieves.

Lulu found herself in difficultly with the law and decided to use a valuable commodity to buy her way out of trouble. She used the information that she had on former Staff Sergeant K, "ratting him out" in order to have her legal problems go away.

Staff Sergeant K was arrested and following a trial he was sentenced to a significant jail term. Lulu then carried on her merry way operating an antique store, which she no doubt used to launder her drug profits. Lulu's actions were frowned on within the drug trade and she did not make herself any friends. So when word began to circulate that someone had taken a contract out on her life, there was no surprise. Whether it was taken out by the corrupt policeman or someone else in the drug trade is not known. Because she was an informant, the R.C.M.P. did take steps to protect her. However, when a young woman was murdered in a store on Lonsdale Avenue in North Vancouver for no apparent reason, it was suspected that Lulu, whose store was next door was the intended target and that the killer had screwed up. The murder of the young woman remains unsolved to this day.

Now the story moves into another phase. Lulu, besides being a thoroughly disreputable person, was also very attractive and had an insatiable sexual appetite, she was constantly on the lookout for virile young men to satisfy her urges. A young policeman from the West Vancouver Police Department had just finished an afternoon shift and decided to go to a pizza joint across the street from the police station, for a beer and a pizza. This tall good looking man was single and so when he was approached by a femme fatale who obviously lusted after his body, who was he to refuse – he felt it was his community duty to assist the "taxpayer" in any way he could. Unfortunately for him, the woman was Lulu and he did not really know much about her. She also owned an antique store in West Vancouver, just a couple of blocks from the restaurant and she invited him to try the antique four poster bed that she had in her store. Away they went, for what I heard to be, a very athletic sexual encounter that tested the springs of the antique bed!

Shortly after this encounter with Lulu, the young police officer was called into a meeting with senior officers and a member of the R.C.M.P. The unfortunate lothario was told about his "lovers" background and of the belief that there was a contract out on her life. It was for this reason, they explained, that Lulus antique shop was wired for sound and that his adventurous evening activities had been captured on audio tape! He was advised to be more cautious in future in his choice of female companionship. Needless to say, he avoided Lulu like the plague. To the best of my knowledge, Lulu never did pay the ultimate price for her betrayal, but continued on with her thoroughly disreputable life style!

The Motorcycle Bandit.

THE 29TH OF June 1984 was a bright sunny day, the Friday before the Canada Day long weekend and most people were feeling good about the approaching holiday. Bob Persowich, an armoured car guard with the Brinks Company, had good reason to be feeling good. He had survived being shot while on duty during a robbery and had just returned to work.

At 4.50 p.m. I was sitting at my desk in the Detective Office, wrapping up my paperwork and anticipating a pleasant weekend with my family. At that moment my telephone rang and I was told that there had been a shooting outside the Government Liquor Store in Park Royal South, a large shopping centre owned by the Guinness family, the Irish brewing conglomerate. While I did not know the seriousness of the incident, I called my wife to tell her that there was a major incident and to expect me home when she saw me. A call that she was used to receiving!

When I arrived at the shopping mall I met with my supervisor, S/Sgt. Henry Indra and Detective Brian Schrierer. They had been in the area and were surveying the scene. Bob Persowich lay dead on the floor of the mall, just outside the Canadian Imperial Bank of Commerce branch that was between the liquor store and the mall exit where the Brinks truck was parked.

The scene of Robert Persowich's murder.

He had been shot three times with a .38 calibre semi-automatic pistol by a person described as a white male 5.10", 160 lbs wearing a full face motorcycle helmet. The killer had then taken the Brinks bag that contained cash from the Government Liquor Store and had fled via an internal stairway that led to the roof top parking. He left the shopping mall on a large motorcycle. Later investigation showed that as Bob Persowich walked out of the liquor store, with the stores takings in a bag, the suspect who had been sitting on the square wooden bench, stood up and fired three rounds from his gun into the back of Bob Persowich. The bullets passed through him and lodged in the wood of the receptionist counter at the entrance to the bank.

Shortly after my arrival at the scene, S/Sgt. Indra assigned me and Detective Colin McKay to head up the investigation. The next year of our lives would be consumed with tracking down the killer and gathering enough evidence to bring him to justice.

Sgt. John Looije was the N.C.O. in charge of the patrol division that day and he directed his uniform members on handling containment of the scene. Two "suspects" on a motorcycle were found in the bush area behind the shopping mall. Both had minor criminal records but I was under no illusion that we had our killer. They were quickly ruled out following an interview.

Bob Persowich was taken by ambulance to the Lions Gate Hospital in North Vancouver and was officially pronounced dead at 5.25p.m. by Dr. C. Creedon in the Intensive Treatment Room.

This stage of a major investigation is an exercise in organized confusion. Detective McKay and I co-ordinated the collection of evidence at the crime scene, the interviewing of witnesses while dealing with an impatient press, who were anxious for a sound bite for the approaching evening news broadcasts. We later established a "Major Incident Room" at the police station. Somewhere that we could use to gather our files, hold meetings and plan our strategy. Today we would use computers to organize the investigation. However, at that time I got my hands on a large ledger book and every detail of the investigation was logged into that book on a daily basis. We would eventually have boxfuls of documents relating to evidence, statements and reports but our logbook was a handy quick reference.

At 9.50 p.m. that night we received a report of an abandoned motorcycle in a bush area just off Moyne Drive in the British Properties, a wealthy residential area of West Vancouver. It was our first break in the case.

We were aware of a bank robber that had been using a similar Modus Operandi (MO) in the Lower Mainland of Vancouver for the past four years. Our first task was to gather information from the other police departments involved to establish if our killer was the bank robber who had become known as the "Motorcycle Bandit". We worked through the night gathering reports from surrounding police departments and planning our strategy. At 5 a.m. Colin McKay went to get some sleep in an empty cell. As my house was only 10 minutes from the police office, I went home to get a couple of hours sleep. At 7 a.m. we both back working on our investigation. While Colin briefed the day shift, who were just coming on duty, I organized our paperwork in preparation for a meeting to be held with the Chief Constable, S/Sgt Indra, Sgt. Frank Aikenhead and other members of the department that would be assisting us in the early days of the investigation when it seemed there were a million things to do.

The day was spent interviewing witnesses and canvassing the residents of Moyne Drive, to establish if they had seen anyone near the motorcycle. Cst. Jim Almas was a dog handler at that time and he did searches in the bush area in case any evidence had been discarded by the suspect as he made his escape. The licence plates from the motorcycle had been removed and the vehicle identification number (VIN) had been chiseled off the machine, making identifying the owner very difficult. At this time we had to link the stolen motorcycle to the murder in order to make the connection in an evidential chain that we need to build. We had some luck when a call was received from the parents of a local paperboy who had been delivering his papers in the area at the time of the murder. He was on a street several blocks north of the shopping mall and he heard a motorcycle coming towards him at high speed. He was interested in seeing the motorcycle so he waited for it to appear. He saw the machine come from a side street and go east on Keith Road. At about that time he heard the sirens as police vehicles converged on the shopping centre. He thought nothing of it until he and his family heard the report of the murder and the suspect escaping on a motorcycle. Keith Road is a dead end street which passes underneath the Trans-Canada Highway and from there the only way any vehicle could go is up the trail that runs on the west side of the Capilano River, this passes by the location that the stolen motorcycle was found. This young man's evidence gave us a critical link to the murderer, we did not realize how critical until the 9th of August 1984.

At the police station, Cst. George Phillipson, the identification officer was dusting the recovered motorcycle for fingerprints and trying to see if any of the erased VIN could be read. As he conducted his examination he removed the seat from the bike and discovered the vehicle registration documents! They were in the tool kit. The murderer had gone to considerable lengths to disguise the true ownership of his means of escape – chiseling the VIN off the machine and removing the licence plate. He never thought of the obvious and failed to check under the seat where many people keep their vehicle registration. He had unwittingly given us another link in our evidentiary chain.

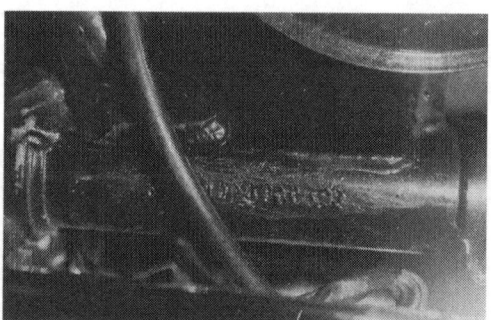

The chiselled off Vin Number on the stolen motor cycle.

Detective Mckay had been making further efforts to link the motorcycle to the murder scene and found marks on a wooden bridge that had been made by the escaping murderer that added to the chain of evidence that would eventually stretch from the shopping centre to the location at which the motorcycle was found.

Detective Colin McKay examines marks left on the bridge by the fleeing motorcycle.

On Sunday, the 01 July 1984 Colin and I came in to work on the case but being the middle of a long weekend there were not many people around the office and it gave us an opportunity to gather our thoughts and follow up on some leads.

There is a tall office tower adjacent to the shopping centre and the top floor was occupied by a government office that monitored the movement of shipping in and around the Vancouver harbour and as far out as the Gulf Islands. An employee who called us mentioned that he had noticed a man standing on the roof of the parking lot that overlooked the entrance to the mall, where the Brinks truck had been parked. As we walked around the scene and determined where the witness had seen the motorcycle, Colin McKay noticed a piece of metal sticking out from the concrete strip that stopped a car's wheels from hitting the wall. He pried it out and discovered the licence place that had been on the stolen motorcycle. Our suspect had obviously taken the plate off the bike as he waited for the Brinks truck to arrive and concealed it. This piece of evidence was very important as it linked the motorcycle found in the bush to the murder scene.

Detective Leishman on Park Royal Roof

We now knew the ownership of the stolen motorcycle and went to Burnaby to interview the owner of the bike. Roy Ocol explained he had advertised his bike for sale and that a man had come to see it on the 2nd June 1984, almost a month before the murder. The man had asked to take the bike for a test drive and gave Ocol a set of car keys, pointing to a car across the street saying it was his. He rode off, never to be seen again and obviously, the keys he had been given were not connected to the car. Roy Ocol was able to give us a description of the man and said he thought he would be able to identify him.

At this point we were now fairly confident that we were dealing with the same suspect who had become known as the "Motorcycle Bandit". The M.O. was very similar in that he also went to see motorcycles that were advertised for sale and took them on a test drive, leaving a set of keys as security. The one difference was that the" Motorcycle Bandit" usually stole his escape vehicle the day before his robbery and then abandoned it without removing licence plates or identification numbers. Our bike was stolen almost a month before the murder and the suspect had gone to great lengths to disguise the true ownership of the vehicle. It seemed fairly obvious that he intended to murder the Brinks guard and had taken extraordinary steps to hide his identity.

The next few days were a flurry of activity. Potential suspects were being identified by various police departments, reports and documents needed to be picked up and witnesses interviewed. Sgt. Frank Aikenhead tried to take some pressure off us and he took responsibility for assigning other detectives to conduct interviews.

In addition to possible suspects being identified by surrounding police departments there was another possibility that we had to consider. A terrorist group that had been identified as the "Squamish Five" had recently been convicted of bank robberies and firearms offences. A copy of the following letter had been sent to the Province Newspaper, who passed it on to police. The original had been found in a photocopy machine in a drug store in Ladysmith, BC.

> Now that the story has been told and the last have been sentenced, it is now that Direct Action will rise again and carry on it's fight against the Capatilists and their projects. This time we will live up to the label of terrorists and urban guerillas given to our predecessors. Unlike them we will move slowly in one direction concentrating on specific goals and striking with calloused devastation. We will not fail. We will stop at nothing. The resurrection of Ann Hansen, Brent Taylor, Gerry Hannah, Julia Belmas, Douglas Stewart and the causes of Direct Action will begin at the start of the Canada Day long weekend. The beginning of the end!
>
> DIRECT ACTION.

Letter linked back to Evans through a typewriter.

The reference to something taking place at the beginning of the Canada Day Long weekend pointed to the murder – no other crimes of similar significance had taken place that weekend. We obtained the letter from the R.C.M.P. in the event that there was a connection.

The funeral for Bob Persowich was on the 5th July 1984 and the media were in full attendance. The noon news showed footage of Kay Persowich, his widow, and her family grieving their loss. While I sometimes find this type of footage intrusive, making a display of a family's grief, in this instance it had a positive effect.

That afternoon a member of the Vancouver Police Department called and gave me the name of a potential witness. This person had called Vancouver police in error but thankfully the VPD member passed this information on. This was our first major break in the case.

Following a brief telephone call with the witness, I drove to their house. This person had a family member that associated with the Motorcycle Bandit, while they were not involved in his crimes they related details to this witness. Like many members of the public, the witness did not want to get involved and ignored the stories that they had heard. However, on this day they had watched the noon news and had been moved by the pictures of the grief stricken Kay Persowich and her family. The witness decided that they just had to do something. I met with the person at their home and Colin Mckay joined me there.

The witness told us that the Motorcycle Bandit was in fact Evan Clifford Evans. He was married to Dianne Evans and they lived in the small town of Ladysmith on Vancouver Island.

Evans was a petty criminal with convictions for minor thefts. However, he had obviously graduated to bank robberies and eventually to the murder of Bob Persowich. Things now began to move at a much more rapid pace. The first thing we needed to do was to obtain an authorization to tap the telephones at Evans home in Ladysmith. That evening Detective McKay and I met with Colin Sweeney, a senior prosecutor with the Regional Crown Counsel, at his office in downtown Vancouver. We met him at 8 p.m. and worked until 12.15 a.m. the following morning to prepare an application for an authorization to intercept private communication. The next morning at 9.30 a.m., I met again with Colin Sweeney to complete the application and it was presented to Supreme Court Judge Randal Wong at 11 a.m. Once I had the signed authorization, The B.C Tel Company were contacted to put the wire taps in place. We began with an interception room at the West Vancouver police station but it soon expanded beyond our capability to monitor it properly and the interception was later moved to the offices of the Co-ordinated Law Enforcement Unit, (CLEU).

At 2.30 p.m. Detective Mckay and I went to the offices of BCTV, a major broadcaster in British Columbia. I had made an appointment with a Mr. Elliot who was the vice president of the organization. We had learned that Evans was a football fan and had been interviewed at a BC Lions game some months earlier. We needed to have some of our witnesses identify Evans and a moving talking video was preferable to a static photo lineup. The purpose of our meeting was to ask the station to give us a copy of the interview. We hoped that they would cooperate but recognized that the media usually did not want to be seen helping the police. I had obtained a search warrant for the TV studios from Justice of the Peace, Mrs. Mary Epps. We felt this would allow them to provide us with the tape without being seen to actively be helping the police.

Mr. Elliot and his news director were hostile from the moment we walked into the meeting. We explained what we wanted and when they said that they did not help police in their investigations, I told them that we recognized that and had brought along a search warrant if that would make things easier. However, things went downhill from there and we had visions of them calling in a camera team and us being featured on the 6 p.m. news. We did not want to alert our suspect that we were on to him. So we walked out of BCTV.

On our return to the office we spoke with Chief Constable Bob Brolly – he picked up the phone and called Frank Griffiths, who owned the station. He would not interfere in the stations operation but assured us that there would be no mention of our visit on the news broadcast. He also said that we could speak with Ray Peters, the Chairman of B.C.T.V. I had to fly to Alberta the next day but on my return I checked the log book and saw a notation written by Detective McKay. "Contacted Ray Peters regarding the tape – Assholes!" Colin McKay's assessment was concise and I heartily agreed. However, things were progressing rapidly in our favour so we could brush that setback aside.

On the day of our meeting with BCTV, I had received a call from Cst. Glenn Motz of the Medicine Hat Police Department in Alberta. A couple had come to their police station and said they knew who the "Motorcycle Bandit" was and that he had murdered the Brinks guard in West Vancouver. I spoke with one of them and while I was not going to reveal who we had identified as the suspect, they told me enough to satisfy me that they did indeed know who had killed Bob Persowich. This had taken place on Friday 06 July 1984 – on Monday the 09th July I flew to Medicine Hat to interview them.

I interviewed this couple and learned that they had known Evans for many years, the female had been a friend of Dianne Evans, his estranged wife. When Evan Evans committed his first bank robbery he had come to speak with the woman before he did the robbery. Evans and his wife had separated and he told her he was doing this robbery at Christmas time so that if he was killed, Dianne would think about it every Christmas! He robbed Deak Perera in Surrey British Columbia on 12 December 1980. I don't know who he thought would kill him – perhaps the frightened cashier that he was pointing a gun at or the housewife behind him with the vicious looking handbag!

I learned that they knew he had committed all the "Motorcycle Bandit" robberies and that he had approached them to set up an alibi for the robbery when he would kill Bob Persowich. He had later changed his plans but now they were fearful that he would come after them because of their knowledge of his robberies. This was their incentive to contact police. I took a full statement from them and they would later give evidence at trial.

Information from intercepted telephone calls that Evans made to his estranged wife in Ladysmith told us that he was staying in Vancouver with someone called Dick, who was later identified as Richard Zess, a bartender at an eastside hotel. Through watching Dick, we eventually found Evans and the next job was to put him under surveillance. The team located Evans on the 10th July 1984 and began following him.

While we were now satisfied that we knew who the killer was, we were a long way from having enough evidence to lay a charge. Evans was put under surveillance by a special team who were specialists at following people. They watched, took photographs and reported back to investigators. Evan Clifford Evans was paranoid about being under police surveillance and took extraordinary measure to try and flush out anyone following him. In one instance in the early days he walked down a dead-end alley and then doubled back. An overeager watcher followed him into the alley too soon and was confronted my Evans – "I guess I blew your cover" he said to the young officer and then walked away. On another occasion he approached an unmarked van with blackened windows and began shaking it, shouting, "I know you are in there". In actual fact a surveillance officer and her partner were hugging the floor of the van as he tried to peer through the blackout windows. Following suspects is not an easy job but for the most part the team never lost him and gathered valuable information.

Evan Clifford Evans captured in a surveillance photo.

The surveillance team had established that Evans was in fact living with a girlfriend, Brenda Sloan who rented a house at on 10th Avenue in Burnaby.

During this time we were having meetings with various police agencies gathering as much intelligence as we could in addition to meeting with Colin Sweeney, the Regional Crown Counsel who had obtained the authorization to tap Evans telephones. Colin had now been assigned to prosecute the case, should we gather enough evidence and he was a valuable source of information for us in exactly what evidence we could use and what we couldn't. At this time I began to compile a "similar fact evidence chart". This would link all the robberies that Evans had committed over the past four years and become valuable evidence to support the murder charge against him.

Similar fact chart

Part way through the trial another robbery that was attributed to Evans was discovered. It had taken place in Langley, British Columbia and in that case one of Evans fingerprints was found on the licence plate of the stolen vehicle.

However, back to the continuing investigation. On the evening of 12th July 1984 we began to have concerns about Evans erratic behaviour. He had again approached a surveillance van with blacked out windows a block from the house on 10th Avenue in Burnaby. We had also learned from wire taps that he planned to travel to Vancouver Island the next day. The decision was made to arrest him when he left the house the following morning.

Following a sleepless night I was at the police station at 5 a.m. on the 13th July 1984. The take down was planned and several scenarios were laid out, depending on which direction he drove off from the house. After seemingly endless hours of waiting in a car a block away, with Detective Colin McKay. At 10.10 a.m. a call came over the radio from Detective Dave Blakeman, of the Vancouver Police Department, part of a joint force operation that were assisting in the arrest, that the suspect was on the move. Despite meticulous planning, the suspect did something we had not planned on. He pulled into the gas station a block away from the house! The decision was instantly made to make the arrest there.

Cars moved in from all sides and as a bewildered Evans stood at the gas pump, he found himself surrounded by armed men and women, handcuffed and being cautioned and read his rights under the Charter, by Detective Dave Blakeman.

The next thing he knew he was in the back seat of a West Vancouver police car, sitting next to Detective Colin McKay, with me behind the wheel. As we drove back to our office he asked where we were from, I replied "West Vancouver". He asked what date it was, I replied, "it is Friday the 13th, do you feel lucky?" It was two weeks to the day since he had murdered Robert Persowich!

At 10.42 a.m. he was booked into the West Vancouver police cell block. I formally told him why he had been arrested, Detective Mckay and Sergeant John Looije, the duty N.C.O. were present.

Now that Evans was in custody, we had to start building a solid case against him. The car he had been driving was towed back to the police station and I found a nylon bag in the back. When it was opened I saw a bundle of money sitting on top of his clothes. Cst. George Phillipson photographed the money as we examined it. When I checked the cash I found two bills with "42" and "43" written on them, the manager of the Liquor Store identified the writing as his he also said the money was bundled as he had bundled the stolen money. Detective McKay found one $20 bill with a serial number that had been recorded in the Liquor Store takings that were stolen from the Brinks guard. This was a very positive link to the murder but not conclusive as Evans explanation at trial was that he had received the money from a drug dealer.

The bag was shown to Evans and asked if it and its contents were his he replied that they were. I then opened the bag and showed him the money, at that time I gave him a warning regarding stolen property and asked him for an explanation as to how it had come into his possession. At that time he told me that he had been advised by his lawyer not to speak with us so he wouldn't. He was returned to his cell.

Cash from the robbery recovered from Evan's bag.

Evan Clifford Evans

While we were making the arrest in Burnaby, other searches were being made at the house in Burnaby and at his wife's home in Ladysmith on Vancouver Island. Detective Dave Weaving was blessed with a very rich brother in law. He borrowed his brother in-laws helicopter to fly over to Ladysmith, I believe it created quite a stir in "little" Ladysmith when a helicopter landed, was met by a police car and the occupants raced off the search the home of Dianne Evans. He and Detective Brian Schierer searched the home and among other things they seized a tool box that belonged to Evans.

The search of the house in Burnaby resulted in the arrest of Brenda Sloan. She was later interviewed by Cpl. Al de Jersey of the R.C.M.P. Cpl. De Jersey had dealt with Brenda Sloan in the past and had developed a rapport with her. She would later give a very informative statement which helped us immensely. However, she feared Evans more than us – she eventually recanted her statement and refused to give evidence on court. But the damage was done, what she told us allowed us to collect much more evidence against him. Brenda Sloan was not familiar with the phrase "loose lips sink ships". She did more than anyone else to sink Evan Clifford Evans ship! As we worked through the investigation Brenda Sloan became an agent for Evans who was being held in custody. She was found in possession of a "key" to a code when she visited him in jail, the idea being that they could pass messages without the authorities being aware of what was being said. Witnesses were coerced and threatened not to give evidence. One young woman was threatened with death and raped in her home, she was told not to go to Evans trial because they thought she would give evidence – in actual fact she had no evidence to give and had not even spoken with the West Vancouver Police. Such was the paranoia of Evans and Brenda Sloan. The young woman's only crime was to have been present in a bar when Sloan was boasting about the activities of her boyfriend, "Heavy Evy!"

However, before Sloan switched back to being an Evans supporter she supplied us with valuable information.

-Evans had told Brenda Sloan that he was going to rob a Brinks guard and that the guard might be killed.

-He discussed the robbery and the murder, after the event with her.

-She told us that his alibi was going to be that he was in Calgary with his wife Dianne

Evans at a football game. They were to stay in The Highlander hotel in Calgary.

-Sloan also told us that he was responsible for the "Direct Action" letter which was designed to "draw the heat away from him."

-She told police that Evans had threatened to kill any informants.

-Brenda Sloan also described her involvement in the robbery of the Toronto Dominion

Bank in Coquitlam on the 21st February 1984. She also disclosed the identity of another young woman who had been a witness to that robbery.

The investigation team now had to begin gathering evidence that would support the information that Brenda Sloan had given us. Cst. Murray Genic of the Coquitlam R.C.M.P. located the young woman, Shirley, who was a witness to the Toronto Dominion Bank robbery. She was a friend of Brenda Sloan and had been taken along when Evans stole the motorcycle he used in that robbery. It was stolen from a man in Richmond, BC. The seller had loaned Evans his helmet for the test ride. Evans later gave it to Shirley who turned it over to Cst. Genic. The owner of the stolen motorcycle was later able to identify the helmet as his. Shirley was also able to say that she was at Brenda Sloan's apartment after the robbery and she helped Sloan and Evans count his loot.

We learned that a member of Dianne Evans family had loaned a typewriter to Evans. Detectives Colin McKay and Ken Banbury travelled to Vancouver Island and seized the typewriter as evidence. While there they also learned from a family member that "Dianne Evans had flown to Calgary to watch a football game with a man called Jose Lazaro, a friend, on the day of the murder".

A line up was held at the Vancouver Police Station, we were able to find a better selection of participants for the lineup in the larger

Evans is number 6 in the lineup.

city. Evans was identified by several people who had been victims of his bank robberies over the past four years. We also had a valuable eye witness who was able to identify Evans at the scene of the murder in Park Royal Shopping Centre. Denise was a young single girl at the time and she worked at Purdy's Chocolates in the mall. She was taking boxes to the garbage and as she walked past the square wooden bench, outside the Liquor Store, she noticed the young man with the motorcycle helmet sitting on the bench. Being a young girl she "checked him out" as she walked by. When she returned he was still there and she took another look at him. Shortly after she had passed him the second time she heard the three gunshots and saw the same man running to the internal stairwell with a gun in one hand and the Brinks bag in the other. Denise was able to identify Evan Clifford Evans in the lineup and became a very valuable witness.

The tool box that Detective Brian Schierer had seized from the home in Ladysmith was taken to the Crime Laboratory a tool marks specialist compared the marks on the stolen motorcycle, where the VIN had been removed, with the tools found in the tool box. On 9th August 1984 we learned that Staff Sergeant Don Watson was able to tell us that a centre punch found in the tool box was used to remove the VIN. The Crime Laboratory was also able to say that the typewriter seized in Ladysmith was the same one used to write the letter purported to be from "Direct Action". The fact that we had found the centre punch in his toolbox was not conclusive, he did not live at the house permanently and could claim it belonged to someone else. We had to link Evans to the toolbox and contents. (These were the finer points that prosecutor, Colin Sweeney, kept us on our toes with.)

Dianne Evans had been attempting to get some of his property released to her, this allowed us to formulate a strategy. The next time Evans was brought to West Vancouver for a court appearance Detective McKay and I took the toolbox containing the tools to a cellblock interview room. We also brought his leather jacket and some other personal items we had seized at the time of his arrest. I then brought Evans to the interview room from his cell and as I walked down the corridor with him I reminded him that he was not obliged to say anything to us and that he was entitled to have counsel present. I had told him we just wanted to check a couple of things with him. As I cautioned him he just brushed it off, saying, "Yea, I know all that stuff".

When we entered the interview room he saw his jacket, the toolbox and several other things. I told him that Dianne wanted to retrieve some of his property and we needed to know if that was alright with him. He picked up some tools from the tool box that were covered in fingerprinting dust and said, "Oh! Do you think I have done some B&Es?" "Well" I replied "we have to check everything". We seized this from Dianne's house in Ladysmith" and now the critical question, "are the tools and the toolbox yours?" "Yes," he replied, "you can let her have them." We returned him to his cell and made copious notes. Two very jolly detectives then treated themselves to a coffee break!

Much activity had taken place and we had made a great deal of progress with the investigation. On the 10th August 1984, Detective McKay and I were able to track down Jose Lazaro at his place of work in Richmond. We introduced ourselves and then told him he was under arrest as an accessory to the first degree murder of Robert

Persowich, and he was duly cautioned. This introduction had the desired effect and he broke down in tears, telling us everything that had taken place. He provided us with a written statement about his involvement. He had been approached by Evans with the offer to have a paid flight to Calgary to provide Evans with an alibi, for what Lazaro thought, would be just another bank robbery. One bonus he thought he was getting was for him to sleep with Evans estranged wife, Dianne. He told us that they went to Vancouver Airport on the day of the murder where Dianne Evans checked them in as Mr. and Mrs. Evans. When they arrived in Calgary they took a taxi to the Highlander Hotel where she again checked them in as Mr. and Mrs. Evan Evans. Lazaro told us that they had tickets for a football game but did not go. He told us that he was in bed with Dianne Evans and she suggested they turn on the television news. When the lead story of the murdered Brinks guard came on, he realized what he had become involved in.

We identified the flight as Canadian Pacific number 56 on the outbound trip on June 29th 1984. The return trip was Canadian Pacific flight 51 on 30th June 1984. We tracked down which seats they had been in and located the people in the adjacent seats. We were able to establish that Evan Clifford Evans was not the man seated next to one of the passenger, he remembered talking with the passenger next to him and was certain it was not Evans.

I then obtained a search warrant for the Highlander Hotel in Calgary and flew there on 7th November 1984 to obtain the hotel records. This was 18 days before my birthday, but I was about to get an early birthday present. When I arrived in Calgary I was met by a Detective Sergeant with the Calgary police force. He accompanied me to the hotel to execute the search warrant for the hotel records. While we were there, the hotel manager produced a letter and said "what am I supposed to do with this?" It was a letter from Richards Israels, a high profile lawyer who was representing Evans. The letter said that Mr. Israels had been instructed by his client, Evan Clifford Evans, that he was a guest at the Highlander Hotel on 29th June 1984 and that he needed a copy of the hotel records to prove this in a court case! Well, we had disproved this alibi and now we had a written confirmation from Evans lawyer that this is what his client had said. Richard Israels had to withdraw as Evans lawyer and we served him a subpoena requiring him to give evidence against Evans at his trial. They fought tooth and nail to avoid this but to no avail. Richard Isreals had to give the evidence in British Columbia Supreme Court.

The preliminary hearing in November and December 1984 was held in the Provincial Court in West Vancouver. Colin Sweeney was the prosecutor and he was assisted by his co-counsel Ms. Mary Tait, another very able prosecutor. During the first several days Brenda Sloan was called as a witness but she refused to testify. She was jailed for contempt for a short period of time but when she continued to refuse she was released. It was during the preliminary hearing that Evans and his lawyer learned that we had linked the centre punch from the tool box to the motorcycle used in the escape by tool marks. It also spoiled their day when I gave my evidence about Evans claiming ownership of the box and tools!

Following that hearing I then charged Evans with 28 counts of armed robbery for which he would be tried later. A murder charge is usually dealt with by itself. After I read the charges to him we took him to the fingerprint room in the cell block. Even though we had his prints, in order to register any additional charges you must fingerprint the suspect for each information that is sworn. At this time he was seething after learning how we had tricked him into admitting ownership of the toolbox and contents. I explained that we needed to print him again and he stepped back into a corner, clenching his fists and said there was no way he was going to let us print him – he was set for a fight! I think he thought the police officers present would pile on him and the fight would be on. However, I decided to handle it differently. I stayed calm and told him if he wanted to do it the hard way that was fine with me. Then in a slow and deliberate manner I took off my jacket, folded it and handed it to someone outside the room, I unloaded my gun and handed that to another officer, asking him to put it in a secure box outside. I then

Chronicles of Tiddly Cove P.D.

Israels & Ballantyne
LAWYERS

RICHARD T. ISRAELS, B.A., M.A., LL.B.
   (ALSO OF MANITOBA BAR)
RICHARD D. BALLANTYNE, B.A., LL.B.

TELEPHONE: 669-9888 24 HOURS
14TH FLOOR, SUN TOWER
100 WEST PENDER STREET
VANCOUVER, B.C.
V6B 1R8

September 7th, 1984

PRIVATE & CONFIDENTIAL

Highlander Hotel
1818 - 16th Avenue N.W.
Calgary, Alta.
T2M 0L8

Attention: Hotel Manager

Dear Sir or Madam:

I have been retained by Mr. E. Evans to act for him in an extremely serious legal matter. His whereabouts on June 29th, 1984, is in dispute and he has instructed us that he and his wife stayed at the Highlander Hotel on June 29th, 1984.

Accordingly I am writing to request written confirmation of same. A xerox copy of the registration that night with a covering letter explaining the significance of the xerox copy would suffice.

This is a matter of grave importance, and your help in this regard is crucial and would be of the greatest value to us. With your informal assistance in this way, further legal action including document subpoenas and involvement of other legal counsel, along with unnecessary court costs can be avoided.

Thank you in advance for your attention to this matter.

Yours truly,

ISRAELS & BALLANTYNE

Richard D. Israels

RDI*re

Letter written by Richard Israels to Highlander Hotel in Calgary, Alberta.

removed my wristwatch and my tie. During this period Evans was mesmerized, not knowing what was going on. I then very quickly sprang at him and handcuffed his hands together before he knew what was happening – he was then fingerprinted by Cst. Andy Mendel without incident. I had remembered what my old Sergeant, Jack Ross, had told me many years ago, "Bullshit baffles brains"

The next few months, leading up to the trial were very busy, court documents had to be served on sensitive witnesses, additional requests for information from Crown Counsel were received and had to be acted on and we found a steady pattern of witness intimidation had begun, Brenda Sloan was at the forefront making telephone calls and threats to witnesses. One turn of events that surprised us was when Dianne Evans called us and wanted to speak with us. She feared that Evans had made an attempt on her life via a second party. She had left the house one day and when she started her car, it burst into flames under the hood. Later examination showed that the fuel line had been disconnected so that when the ignition was turned on gasoline sprayed under the hood, when the spark plugs sparked the fuel ignited. She could only think that Evans had turned on her and had an associate booby trap her car. While she did speak with us, there was little that she could tell us that we did not already know. Because they were still married, she would not have been able to give evidence against him. She did tell us that Evans got his guns from a man in Squamish called Oliver Plunkett. He was very likely the person who sabotaged Dianne Evans car. I will tell you more about Plunkett at the end of this story.

I mentioned earlier that Brenda Sloan had told us about a young woman who had been present at the time of the bank robbery in Coquitlam. Shirley was to be a witness regarding that case, during the similar fact evidence that was being used in the murder trial. Shirley was being harassed and threatened by Brenda Sloan and she was terrified. We relocated Shirley in another city until the time of the trial. Brenda Sloan had also convinced Jose Lazaro to change his story and had taken him to a meeting with Evans lawyer. While inconvenient, it was not critical to the case as we had all the supporting evidence and his written statement.

When Colin Mckay and I had a spare moment, which wasn't very often, we turned the tables on Brenda. We would park our car down the block from her house and wait until she spotted us. We would then just drive away. However, because Sloan was paranoid, she thought she was under surveillance around the clock and was constantly checking over her shoulder, no matter where she went. If it caused her some inconvenience and stress, that was alright with us!

The trial was held in the Supreme Court of British Columbia and lasted for eight weeks. The defence fought very hard to have various pieces of evidence excluded. However, because of the high standards that Colin Sweeney and Mary Tait had held McKay and me to, all the evidence was admitted.

Evans defence was that he was actually a drug dealer and that when Jose Lazaro and Dianne Evans went to Calgary, it was actually to do a drug deal on his behalf. In regards to the stolen money found in his possession from the Persowich murder, he claimed to have received that from a man for drugs. It was his contention that the "mystery man" must have robbed the Brinks guard and passed the money along to him for drugs. He had a very able lawyer, who had replaced Richard Israels, and they foot tooth and nail to discredit varies pieces of evidence. However, at the end of the day, the jury found him guilty of first degree murder and he was sentenced to life in prison, with no eligibility for parole for 25 years. He served the full term of 25 years and was recently released on parole.

In conclusion a few comments on Oliver Plunkett and Evans early days in prison. Plunkett was a supplier of guns to criminals and had supplied Evans with the two guns he used in his string of robberies and the murder of Robert Persowich. Shortly before the trial had ended I found myself investigating the death of Oliver Plunkett. He jumped to his death from the Lions Gate Bridge and this was witnessed by the sister of his deceased wife. I learned the following facts from Cst. Julio Krenz of the Squamish R.C.M.P.

Plunkett and his late wife were having disputes about domestic affairs and Krenz had learned from an informant that Evans thought that Plunkett's wife was the person who informed on him. One evening, Plunkett drove into the Squamish hospital, his wife was in the front seat of the car, dead from a bullet through the back of her head. His story was that they were driving on a dark stretch of highway when a car drove up behind them and started flashing its lights. He claimed he thought it was a police car and pulled over. As they sat in the car Plunkett said someone walked up to the open passenger window and shot his wife through the head. He said the car then drove away and he could not give a description! It would appear that for whatever reason, Plunkett had murdered his wife and eventually could not live with himself. There were no tears shed in the police community!

Following his conviction, Evans began serving his life sentence in Kent Federal Prison. Some months later I received word through the prison security that Evans had taken a contract out on the life of Shirley Earl. He had paid Michael Dapic, a prisoner about to be released on parole, to kill her. Brenda Sloan was supposed to track Shirley down for him. We moved quickly and Shirley was relocated to Eastern Canada under a witness protection program. Dapic could not find Shirley and spent the money he had been paid on drugs. His parole was later revoked and he was returned to Kent Prison. Evans, not being able to go to the consumer protection branch for breach of contract, apparently beat him very badly, almost killing him. I am sure you can sense the heartache I felt.

Sometime later Evans accepted a contract himself and murdered Randy Sexsmith, who coincidently was in jail for robbing a West Vancouver bank. He stabbed Sexsmith to death in a cell and when caught leaving the cell covered in blood, he claimed that he had been passing by when he saw Sexsmith laying dying in the cell. He said he had gone in to "comfort" him and while he held him the dying man was writhing around in his death throes. That accounted for the scratches and blood on him!

So far so good. However, at the autopsy the pathologist found that of the multiple stab wound, one had severed his spine and after that wound was received, there could not have been any movement from Sexsmith. Evans was charged with the murder but another inmate gave evidence under the "protection of The Canada Evidence

Act" claiming that he had murdered Sexsmith. Because of how he had given his evidence he could not be prosecuted for the murder. That raised a reasonable doubt and Evans was acquitted.

He was tried on all the robbery counts by crown prosecutor Joe Bellows and convicted but his sentence was concurrent to his life sentence. While this case was just one of many that I investigated, it was certainly the biggest and it kept Detective Colin McKay and me working very hard for over a year. However, we both felt a great deal of satisfaction that, with the help of other team members, we had been able to track down this vicious killer and build a case good enough for Colin Sweeney and Mary Tait to obtain a conviction.

Conclusion

This concludes my book. I do hope that you have enjoyed reading it as much as I enjoyed writing it. For any of my former colleagues who read this book – it is unfortunate that I could not mention you all and the contributions you made to the many investigations undertaken by the West Vancouver Police Department. A police department is reflected by the quality of its members, civilian and sworn. While I won't pretend that the organization was perfect, there were some "Uriah Heep" (Charles Dickens, not the rock band) type of characters who were more interested in climbing the slippery pole of promotion than in the success of the department. However, these people were in the minority. Our civilian staff over the years were outstanding as well as the majority of the uniform and plain clothes members. The citizens of West Vancouver are well served by their own police department and I hope they never, willingly, let it go.

I would be very happy to hear from any of my readers with comments, suggestions or questions. I can be contacted at mybookcomments@gmail.com.

About the Author

Stuart Leishman was born at an early age, in Yorkshire, England. At the age of eleven he lived in Spain with the Yoldi family, while their eldest son, Pedro, lived with his family in Halifax, West Yorkshire for one year.

School was followed by work in the hotel industry, beginning with The Old Swan Hotel in Harrogate, Yorkshire. At age 19 he moved to Saskatchewan, Canada with his younger brother where he worked as an "iceman" in a curling rink, a hotel waiter and then sales. He returned to England to marry and then exposed his new wife to several frigid prairie winters before the warmer climate of British Columbia beckoned them west.

They moved to North Vancouver and have lived there to this day, raising a son (a policeman with the Vancouver Police) and now enjoying two wonderful grandchildren.

Stuart worked in the trucking industry for several years before joining the West Vancouver Police Department on September 1st 1973. When he worked as a detective he spent a significant amount of time working on cases of child sexual assault and was one of the pioneers in using video tape while interviewing the young victims. This reduced the number of times that the victims had to recount their ordeal. A well conducted interview on video often resulted in a guilty plea once the accused and his lawyer had reviewed what the child would say in court.

Working with victims of sexual abuse led to Stuart writing a book, The Child Sexual Assault Manual, for the West Vancouver Police Association. He received eight Chief Constables Commendations during his career. After retirement he was approached by the British Columbia Police Federation to begin publication of a magazine, The Thin Blue Line. He was the Editor of this magazine for six years before passing the reins along to another retired Police Officer, Ole Jorgensen.

Now retired, he passes his time writing and travels extensively with his wife either in their motorhome or on cruise ships.

Made in the USA
Lexington, KY
21 March 2019